Nan.

1000 Things
You Ought to Know

Ginette Chevallier

1000 Things You Ought to Know

Illustrated by Malcolm Bird

JILL NORMAN

Jill Norman Ltd, 90 Great Russell Street, London WC1B 3PY

First published 1980
Copyright © Airtrans Establishment 1980
Illustrations copyright © Malcolm Bird 1980

British Library Cataloguing in Publication Data
Chevallier, Ginette
   1000 things you ought to know.
   1. Home economics
   I. Title II. Thousand things you ought to know
   640   TX145

ISBN 0-906908-02-7

Printed in Great Britain by
W & J Mackay Limited, Chatham

To my boyfriend . . . my husband!

Contents

Preface

This book really began with a power cut.

One evening I was having dinner with my boyfriend and some guests at his home when all the lights went off quite suddenly. The whole street being in darkness, we realised that the fault was not in the house.

As he was a confirmed bachelor (I was in my fifth year of waiting for him to make up his mind whether or not to marry me!) my boyfriend's household was not organised to the point where one could find candles or any other form of lighting in an emergency. So I quickly went into the kitchen, filled a glass two-thirds full with water, topped it with a thin layer of salad oil, cut a thick ring from a wine cork and made a hole in the middle of it. Through the hole in the cork I slid a wick I had made from cotton thread found in a kitchen drawer. I floated the cork on top of the oil, lit the wick and returned to the diningroom, much applauded and admired for this little 'tour de force'. 'How did you do it?' It was so simple that I thought everybody knew about it.

I was just being practical. Being practical is very useful and most rewarding, especially when your child returns from school with ink over his new shirt and you can keep smiling, knowing that lemon juice will take care of it. Or knowing that a few drops of vinegar in the water when you are cooking cabbage will stop the unpleasant smell filling the whole house. Or knowing that marigold petals can replace the expensive saffron in your rice or other dishes most successfully. Or that a few dabs of your favourite scent around the hem of your skirt will surround you with a lovely smell every time you move.

So, after my little experience at the dinner party I started to gather ideas and information: from personal experience, from my family, from my friends, from years of visits to the British Museum Library, from libraries in France. In all, a thousand simple ideas and pieces of information which, I hope, will help you the way they have been helping, and still help, many thousands of people everywhere in their daily life. It is the simple things that work best.

PS. Two weeks after the power cut my boyfriend asked me to marry him – I did.

I would like to thank my editors for the invaluable help they gave me all the way through this book.

The Kitchen

Cooking

Almonds

To skin almonds, pour boiling water over them and allow to stand for 3 to 4 minutes. Drain and then rub the almonds between your fingers – the skin will come off very easily.

Anchovies

To remove excess salt, and to make anchovies moist, soak them in milk for 4 to 5 hours or, even better, overnight.

Apples

Apples will peel more easily if you first pour scalding water over them and allow them to stand for a few minutes.

Apple stains

To remove stains from your hands after peeling a large quantity of apples, just rub the stains with apple peel and then wash your hands.

Arrowroot

Use arrowroot instead of flour for thickening sauces and gravies, and making sweet dishes. It is a much finer and more digestible starch than flour, and is particularly suitable as a food for young children and people with delicate stomachs. Blend the arrowroot with a small quantity of cold liquid before adding to the hot soup, sauce, etc., and always stir it into the dish off the heat. Arrowroot is good when making clear sauces as it becomes transparent when cooked.

Artichokes (globe)

A perfect globe artichoke has tight leaves, and is heavy and firm. If the leaves are open, the artichoke will be tough and tasteless.

If you intend to keep your artichokes for a few days before cooking them, stand them in a vase with the stems in the water like a bunch of flowers. Renew the water and cut ½ inch (1 cm) off the stem every day.

When cooking artichokes, put a few drops of lemon juice or vinegar in the cooking water to bring out the flavour.

Never keep a cooked artichoke for more than a day, even in the refrigerator. Because of its iron content it becomes toxic when exposed to the air for a prolonged period.

Asparagus

Fresh asparagus should be firm and should break cleanly when bent. The best time to buy it is in March and April: at the end of the season it becomes bitter, and you should leave the spears in cool water for a few minutes after cooking.

To keep asparagus fresh for a few days, wrap it in a wet cloth.

Aubergines

Sliced or diced aubergines are best if sprinkled generously with salt and left for 30 minutes. This will remove any excess liquid and any bitterness. Before cooking them, rinse off the salt and dry with a paper towel. Aubergine tends to soak up oil when fried, but you will find it needs less oil after this treatment.

Avocados

When buying an avocado which is to be eaten the same day, press the stalk end: if it is soft, the fruit is ripe. Never buy an avocado with dark spots: it is too ripe. To ripen a hard avocado, leave it in the kitchen or a warm place until soft.

To store a cut avocado, brush the flesh with lemon juice to prevent it going brown. Leave in the stone, and cover tightly with plastic cling wrap.

Bacon

Choose bacon in which the lean is a pinky brownish colour and the fat is evenly distributed. The rind should be thin.

Bananas

The best bananas are from the Canary Islands – they are very curved, and smaller than other varieties. Bananas from America are fatter and have less flavour.

Do not store bananas in the refrigerator as their skins turn black if kept too cold.

Barbecues

Line the base and sides of your barbecue with aluminium foil, shiny side up, to intensify the heat.

Meat should be brushed with oil before being placed on the barbecue grill, and more oil should be applied during cooking. The grill should also be oiled.

Marinate the meat before barbecuing. This will improve and tenderise cheaper cuts of meat.

Basil

Grow basil on your kitchen windowsill in pots to keep flies away.

Basil leaves keep their flavour best when preserved in oil. Put cleaned leaves into a container, sprinkle with salt, shake the container and then fill with olive or vegetable oil. Cover the container and leave in the refrigerator, where it will last for months. Remove a few leaves when needed.

Bay leaves

Press bay leaves under a board and then dry them in a dark room, not in the sun. When dry, store them in a dark container such as a cardboard box (not in a glass jar).

Beans

Dried beans should be soaked before cooking. Newly dried beans will need 2 hours' soaking; older ones will need between 6 and 8 hours. Do not over-soak for this causes the beans to ferment and germinate, making them difficult to digest.

If you don't have time to soak them, use the following method. Put the beans into cold water, bring to the boil, and throw the water away. Repeat this process three times. After the third boiling, keep the water and cook the beans in it.

Do not add salt until the end of the cooking time, or the beans will harden.

Beef

Choose meat which is slightly marbled with fat, a sign that the animal has been well fed. The fat should be a creamy colour and firm to the touch; the lean should be bright red.

Grilling

The perfect way to cook red meat is to grill it until slightly bloody, and then let it rest for a few minutes before serving. This allows the juices which have gathered in the centre of the meat during the cooking to reach the edges, and the meat will be pink throughout. If it is not done, the grilled piece of meat will be flabby and too rare in the middle, the outside having a blackish crust a few millimetres thick.

To test beef, prick with a skewer. If a very light pink juice runs out, the meat is cooked.

Beef to be eaten cold should not be sliced while hot.

Beef broth (pot au feu)

When making beef broth, line the base of the pan with bones and put the meat on top so that it will not stick. Cover with cold water and bring to the boil slowly to keep the meat tender and palatable. (Put a thick slice of carrot at each end of a marrow bone to prevent the marrow falling out.) Vegetables do not all have the same consistency, so do not cook them for the same length of time or they will become tasteless. Cook turnips for 40 minutes, carrots for 30 minutes and leeks for 10 minutes. This is the way to a successful broth.

See also *Meat* on page 35.

Beer

When cooking with beer, use it warm; if chilled it loses most of its flavour.

Left-over beer can be used for cooking if you put a little sugar or a few grains of rice in the bottle before corking it tightly. This stops it going flat.

Do not be afraid of giving food cooked in beer or wine to children. The alcohol evaporates and only the delicious flavour remains.

Instead of red wine in meat dishes use Guinness: it is cheaper and gives a slightly nutty flavour. Replace white wine with cider. (Reduce the cider by boiling it before adding to the dish.)

Beetroot

If beetroot is bruised, rub the cut or bruised part with salt. This will prevent it bleeding and losing its colour when boiled.

Beetroot has more flavour and is more nutritious if roasted in the oven rather than boiled.

To keep beetroot red when it is being boiled, add a little bicarbonate of soda to the water.

To peel hot beetroot, put it into cold water and the skin will peel off like a glove.

Blackcurrants

These are richer in Vitamin C than any other fruit, and are also very rich in Vitamin A.

Use a fork to strip blackcurrants from their stalks.

Bones

Keep any bones and carcases from chicken, duck, goose, turkey or roast meat and store them in a big plastic bag in the freezer for when you want to make soup. They will keep in the freezer for 1 month. After using the bones to make stock, give them to chickens to pick as they are helpful in the production of egg-shells.

Bouillon

When making bouillon, always add some minced meat as it gives a better flavour.

Before storing, pour the bouillon through a fine strainer or muslin (the vegetables would ferment very rapidly). Boil the strained bouillon once more and then leave it to cool, uncovered, before pouring into a container.

Bouquet garni

Fresh: use 1 bayleaf, 2 sprigs of parsley and 1 sprig of thyme, tied together with cotton.

Dried: use 1 bayleaf, 2 pinches of mixed herbs (thyme, marjoram and parsley), 5 peppercorns and 2 cloves.

The mixture should be tied in a small square of muslin, with a piece of cotton long enough to tie to the handle of the pan; or put it in a perforated spoon of the sort used for infusing tea.

Bread

To re-heat bread, use a lukewarm oven for 20 to 30 minutes rather than a very hot oven. This method allows you to re-heat the bread meal after meal if necessary.

Use left-over bread to make French toast. For one person you need 2 slices of bread, 1 egg, ¼ pint (150 ml) of milk, 2 level tablespoons of sugar, and a walnut-sized knob of butter. Cut the crust from the bread, dip each slice in the milk (to which the sugar has been added) and then in the beaten egg. Melt the butter in a pan and place the slices in the hot butter. Fry each side until a light golden-brown, and serve hot with brown sugar – a very nourishing and delicious tea snack.

Browning

You do not have to use browning to colour bouillon. An onion boiled in its skin gives a lovely dark colour.

Brussels sprouts

Trim off the damaged outer leaves, but do not cut the ends. Simmer the sprouts uncovered in a little water for 10 to 12 minutes, after which they will be crisp and still green.

Butter

If butter starts to burn during cooking, add a little cooking oil.

Clarified butter

When clarified, butter burns less readily. To make clarified butter, melt ordinary butter over a low heat and skim off the foam that rises to the top. A white residue will sink to the bottom. Strain the clear yellow butter and discard the white residue.

Cabbage and cauliflower

A few drops of vinegar or a piece of stale bread added to the water in which you are cooking cabbage or cauliflower will absorb the smell. A small peeled onion will also work wonders.

Cakes

When baking a cake (e.g. a fruit cake) which requires long cooking, place the tin containing the cake in another tin a size or two bigger. This will prevent the cake burning. Another method is to place a dish of water in the lower part of the oven, beneath the cake.

Cream butter and sugar together, and then add part of the flour *before* the liquid to prevent the butter congealing. Add the remaining flour and liquid alternately, beating thoroughly.

To test a cake, press it with your finger. If it leaves a mark, the cake is not cooked. To make sure, insert a skewer into the centre of the cake: if the skewer comes out clean, the cake is cooked.

When icing a cake, first sprinkle a little flour over the top of the cake to stop the icing running over the sides.

When baking a cake without shortening (e.g. a sponge cake), sprinkle the tin with flour but do not grease it.

A light sponge cake is generally baked in a tin greased with melted cooking fat or oil and dusted lightly with flour.

To protect a heavy cake from the high temperature in the oven, line the bottom and sides of the tin with greased paper.

Caramel

To prevent caramel going hard, add a little lemon juice.

Carrots

When scraping carrots, use a wire pot-scourer: it is quicker and more effective than using a knife.

Carrot juice

If you do not have an electric blender or liquidiser, scrub and clean the carrots well; peel them if they are old, scrape them if young. Then put a grater over a clean cloth, grate the carrots, and extract the juice by squeezing the grated carrots in the cloth. If you do have an electric blender, pass the carrots through a piece of muslin after blending. Honey can be added for sweetness or parsley for flavour.

Carrot juice contains Vitamins A, B and C, iron, iodine and calcium. Its natural sugar gives energy. It also improves eyesight.

Cauliflower

See Cabbage and Cauliflower on page 19.

Celery leaves

Don't discard celery leaves: use them in a salad, or dry them for use in soups, sauces and stews. Add them at the end of the process and do not cook them for more than a few minutes.

Cheese

Cheese is a very important source of protein: 1 lb (about 500 g) of a hard cheese such as Cheddar provides as much protein as 2 lb (about 1 kg) of beef.

The transparent wrapping in which pre-packed cheese is sold causes the cheese to sweat in a warm atmosphere, so remove the plastic,

wrap the cheese in aluminium foil and keep it in the refrigerator. If you store it in a cold larder, cover it loosely with a cloth damped in vinegar to protect it from the air. Keep the cloth permanently damp.

To keep cheese free of mould, place a lump of sugar on it. This will keep it fresh and absorb the moisture.

Furry cheese is safe to eat: the fur is caused by fermentation, and may simply be cut off.

Don't forget that cheese, like red wine, should be served at room temperature, so take it out of the refrigerator at least 1 hour before it is needed.

Cheese melts at a fairly low temperature, so if you are browning the top of a savoury cheese dish, place it under a fairly low grill or the cheese will become tough, stringy and indigestible.

Cheese for cooking

Gruyère has a strong flavour and is very tasty; it is perfect for soufflés, croquettes and fondues.

Parmesan makes soups velvety and is very good for sauces, soufflés, and Italian dishes such as risotto, minestrone and pasta.

Emmenthal is very rich, and adds a delicious, mild flavour to a dish.

Tilsit melts quickly; it makes pizza, fondue or toppings very smooth.

Cream cheese cannot usually be frozen, but Kraft Philadelphia cream cheese will freeze successfully.

To make use of bits and pieces of left-over cheese (Cheddar, Stilton, Brie, Camembert), mix them in the blender with 2 tablespoons of fresh cream. Put this mixture into an earthenware jar and serve like Stilton at the table, or make it a little creamier and serve as a dip or on celery stalks with drinks.

Chestnuts
Before cooking chestnuts under the grill or in the oven, make a slight incision in the skin to stop them bursting.

Chicken
See *Poultry* on page 43.

Chicory
Trim and wash broad-leafed chicory rapidly under cold running water. Do not leave the chicory standing in the water as this makes it bitter.

Chips
Chips can be prepared a little while in advance of a meal. Half cook the chips in hot oil or fat, then drain them and keep until they are needed. At this stage, dip them for the second time into hot oil or fat until golden, drain on kitchen paper, sprinkle with salt and serve immediately.

Chutney
For a quick chutney, take some smooth apricot jam, add vinegar to taste and a pinch of cayenne pepper.

Coconut
To crack a coconut easily, first pierce the eyes with a large nail, drain the juice, and then put the coconut in the oven (325°F, 170°C, Gas

Mark 3) for half an hour. When it cools it will probably crack open by itself; if not, tap it lightly with a hammer.

When choosing a coconut, shake it to find out if it contains any milk. A good coconut should be heavy. Avoid the ones with wet eyes.

Coffee

For good coffee, never boil either the coffee or the milk.

Iced coffee will taste better and be stronger if you pour the brew of hot coffee and milk into tall glasses half filled with coffee ice-cubes.

Coffee ice-cubes

Freeze freshly made coffee of double or treble the normal strength in the ice-cube tray of the refrigerator.

Cold plates

Do not spoil your meal by forgetting to heat your dinner plates.

Cream

Double cream whips best if the cream and the bowl are refrigerated beforehand, and if 1 tablespoon of milk is added to every ¼ pint (150 ml) of cream.

Single cream will not whip, however hard you try.

Whipped cream

Do not over-beat or the cream will turn into butter. As soon as the cream becomes stiff, stop whipping – it is ready. The mixture can be stored in the refrigerator until needed.

Crème anglaise

To find out if the cream is cooked, plunge a cold spoon into it. After taking it out draw a line on it with your finger; if the two sides stay apart the cream is ready. Always keep a container of cold water on the side so that you can stop the cooking by dipping the pan in it.

Cucumber

Avoid indigestion when eating fresh cucumber by cutting it a few hours before it is required. Sprinkle it with salt and leave to drain. The drained-off liquid is the cause of the trouble.

Currants

Currants should be washed and dried in a cloth before use; if damp, they will make cakes or puddings heavy. A dusting of flour on the currants will make your cakes lighter and stop the fruit sinking to the bottom.

Currants contain iron and provide roughage which helps regularity, and they play an important part in preventing acid conditions of the blood. One pound (about 500 g) of dried currants has all the food value of 3½ lb (about 1¾ kg) of grapes. Currants are a healthy snack for children's school breaks.

Dried fruit

See *Fruit* on page 29.

Dandelion

Common dandelion can be found almost anywhere – in water meadows or dry hills. Its young leaves make a delicious salad: add a touch of garlic and mustard vinaigrette. Dandelion is also considered a blood cleanser.

Dripping

To separate dripping from fat, put it in a basin and pour boiling water over it. The next day the fat will have formed into a cake on top of the water. Remove the cake, in one piece if possible, and repeat the process three times. You will get beautifully purified dripping.

A delicious way of collecting dripping from grilled steaks, chops, ham and other meat is to place on a sheet of foil underneath them slices of bread which have been well toasted on one side. Place the toasted side down and the dripping will soak into the bread, the toasted lower side preventing the juices from passing through.

Duck

Stuff duck or goose with 2 unpeeled apples to soak up the fat. (Do not eat the apples afterwards.)

For very crisp roast duck, the skin must be very dry. In the winter hang the bird for at least 4 hours in an airy spot, or leave it to dry overnight; or douse the bird with boiling water, dry it thoroughly with a towel or kitchen paper; or try drying the bird with a hairdryer – the drier the crisper – before putting it in the oven.

See also *Poultry* on page 43.

Eggs

White shell or brown shell? Eggs must be bought clean, as the shell is porous and allows germs to penetrate. Brown shells are thicker and less porous than white shells.

Eggs are fresh if, when placed in a bowl of cold water, they sink straight to the bottom and stay there; if they float they are not fresh. If they tilt between the two they can be used for pastries. To test for freshness you can also place your tongue on the end of the egg: a new egg will feel warm, whereas an old egg will feel quite cold. Or shake the egg by your ear: a fresh egg will not make any noise, an old one will.

To preserve new-laid eggs, smear the shells with pure glycerine on the day they are laid; at the end of a few weeks they will be just as fresh. If possible, store eggs with the small end upwards. They will keep for a month if you boil them for 1 minute.

Fresh eggs tend to take a little longer to cook than those that are a few days old, as do eggs coming straight from the refrigerator.

Hens' eggs should be lightly cooked. Prolonged cooking toughens the white and makes it less digestible.

Duck eggs do not keep fresh for very long because they have a very porous shell. They can be contaminated by germs from the duck, so they should be thoroughly cooked to be safe – for at least 12 to 14 minutes. They should not therefore be used in lightly cooked dishes, but cooked at temperatures high enough to kill any germs that have been present. They should not be preserved.

Goose eggs are larger than hens' eggs, but they are as delicate in flavour and can be cooked in as many different ways. One goose egg is the equivalent of three hens' eggs. Cook 7 minutes for a soft-boiled egg, 14 minutes for a hard-boiled egg.

Gull, plover and pheasant eggs are usually eaten hard-boiled and can be served as an hors d'œuvre. (Cook for 10 to 15 minutes.)

Cooking time for hens' eggs varies according to the size of the eggs, but on average the time is as follows:
2 minutes – very soft-boiled egg with creamy white and slightly liquid yolk.
3 minutes – soft white, very soft yolk.
3½ minutes – well-done white, soft yolk.
5 minutes – very well-done white, well-done yolk.
6 minutes – very well-done white, thick yolk.
10 minutes – hard-boiled egg.

The perfect way to boil an egg is to bring the water to the boil, put the egg in it and then remove the saucepan from the heat. Leave the egg in the water for 6 minutes. This method prevents the white from becoming leathery, and is also very economical. Leave the egg for a few minutes longer if you prefer it more cooked.

When an egg cracks in boiling water, quickly put in a teaspoon of vinegar to prevent the white from running; if the white is already escaping, put a teaspoon of salt in the water.

Before putting a cracked egg into water, wrap it very tightly in tissue paper (screw the ends in opposite directions) and it will not boil out of its shell.

When cutting hard-boiled eggs, dip the blade of your knife in hot water beforehand to prevent them breaking.

When poaching an egg, add a little vinegar to the water to prevent the egg breaking.

A delicious way of poaching an egg is to put a small piece of butter into a cup, stand the cup in a little boiling water in a pan, break the egg into it and steam for 7 to 9 minutes.

Eggs continue to cook in the pan when it is removed from the heat. When making scrambled eggs, fried eggs or omelettes, take the pan off the heat before they are quite ready and let them finish cooking in the pan.

When separating an egg, break it into a funnel: the white will run through and the yolk will remain.

When the white only is needed, separate the egg in the usual way and put the yolk into a container. Cover it with cold water and keep in the refrigerator. When needed, drain off the water. The yolk will stay perfectly fresh for several days.

When beating the white of an egg, add a small pinch of salt; it will whip better and faster. If possible, don't whip an egg white when the egg is cold from the refrigerator. You do not get the same volume from a cold egg.

Fat

If fat catches fire in the kitchen, *do not* pour water over it; cover the pan with flour or kitchen salt.

Do not pour fat down the sink. If you do, it will solidify and block the drain. If you have done so inadvertently, pour boiling water down the sink immediately.

Figs

When dried figs become too dry, steam them until they soften.

Fish

Fish must be very fresh; this is most important. Gills should be pink or bright red. If there are scales, they should be bright and silvery. Eyes should be clear and prominent, the flesh should be firm, and there should be a pleasantly fresh smell. When cut, the flesh should be creamy and not too transparent. If the scales rub off, the gills are pale, the eyes sunken and the whole fish flabby then it is stale.

Fish to be thawed in a hurry can be put, sealed in its wrapping, in cold water (not warm). The slower a fish thaws, the less juice it will lose.

Fish thawed in its wrapping in the refrigerator takes about 8 hours per pound (about 500g). It takes half as long if thawed at room temperature.

Fish cooked when still frozen takes longer to cook than if thawed first, and it must be cooked at a lower temperature.

Fish fried in an aromatic beer batter is delicious, as is a beer sauce on plain grilled or boiled fish.

When scaling a fish is difficult, dip it for a few seconds into boiling water.

When cooking a fish, the slim part can be protected by sliding a slice of potato under the tail. This should be done when the fish is partly cooked.

For fish without smell, clean the fish but leave on the scales. Bury it without seasoning in 4 lb (about 2 kg) of coarse salt and cook for an hour in the oven. Serve with lemony butter – delicious. Cook for only half an hour when using sardines.

When grilling a fish, do not scale it beforehand. The scales protect the fish from the high temperature and keep the flesh soft and tasty. Skin and scales come off easily at the end of cooking.

To test if a fish is cooked, pull out one of the small bones near the head. If it comes out easily, the fish is ready.

When poaching a fish to be eaten cold, leave it to cool in the cooking water.

Fish smells

To remove fish smells in a pan, put 1 teaspoon of methylated spirit in the pan, strike a match and burn the spirit. Rinse well afterwards. (Make sure that you put the bottle of methylated spirit back in the cupboard before starting this little operation.)

Another method of getting rid of fish smells is to boil coffee grounds in the pan in which the fish has been cooked.

To remove the smell of fish from silverware, add a spoonful of mustard to the washing-up water.

To remove the smell of fish from your hands, rub them with mustard.

Flour

When flour is milled, the whole grain is broken up and separated, sifted, blended and ground into flour. Some of the bran is removed, as is the wheatgerm which contains oil and could go rancid. Because the bran and the wheatgerm are left in wholemeal flour it cannot be stored for long (2 months). The finer and whiter the flour, the less its food value as more of its nutritious content has been removed.

True wholemeal and whole wheatmeal flours contain 100 per cent of the whole grain. Wheatmeal flour contains 85–90 per cent of the whole grain. White flour contains 72–74 per cent of the whole grain. Self-raising flour contains 72–74 per cent of the whole grain, plus bicarbonate of soda and cream of tartar.

If flour is sifted two or three times before use, cakes will be much lighter.

Flour should always be mixed with *cold* liquid or it will go lumpy.

Freezer

In case of a breakdown or power cut, food will keep for 24 hours if the freezer is not opened. Lumps or bags of dry ice (carbon dioxide) put in the top of the freezer will help to keep the food frozen longer, as will layers of newspapers or blankets.

Freezing liquid

To freeze liquid in a plastic bag, first put the bag into a box then pour the liquid into the bag and place it in the freezer. When frozen, remove the box and the liquid inside the bag will have taken the shape of the box, making it easier to store in the freezer.

Frozen food

When buying frozen food, always have with you some newspapers in which you can wrap the food to insulate it. Once home, the food should be put straight into the freezer.

Do not re-freeze packets of frozen food once they have thawed.

Fruit

Fruit such as apples, pears, peaches and pineapples, once cut for fruit salad or other uses, should be covered at once with lemon or lime juice to prevent discolouration.

To speed the ripening process, place fruit in closed paper bags in a warm place.

Dried fruit should be washed in boiling water. Discard the water, cover again with boiling water and soak overnight. The next day, bring the fruit to the boil in the same water with or without sugar to taste.

Fruit juice

Fresh fruit juices should always be drunk immediately they are prepared as they lose some of their vitamins and their flavour if exposed to the air for any length of time.

For juices made from soft fruit, lemon should always be added immediately to retain the colour.

Frying

When frying fat has burned slightly, a raw peeled potato dropped into the pan for a few minutes and then removed will take all trace of burning away.

Game birds

When fresh, game birds should have legs that are pliable and smooth, feet that are supple, and prominent eyes. In young birds, the part under the beak is brittle.

When buying a game bird, ask whether it has been hung. For game to be tender and to develop its distinctive taste it needs to be hung without being plucked or drawn. The length of hanging time is a matter of individual taste and weather – from a week in hot weather to 2 to 3 weeks in cold, frosty weather. Hang the bird by the legs in an airy, cold, dry place.

To keep flies away while game is hanging, sprinkle the bird with a mixture of ground pepper, ground cloves, and flour.

Garlic

Unpeeled garlic cloves give a lighter flavour. Use the whole cloves in soups, stock, stew, sauces, etc., but do not forget to remove the clove or cloves before serving.

If you find garlic indigestible, cut the clove in half and remove the germ from the middle before use.

Before peeling a clove of garlic, press it firmly between your fingers or under the flat blade of a knife until you hear a crack. The skin will then come off easily.

See also *Salad dressing* on page 45.

Geranium leaves and flowers

Jams, jellies, sweet stewed fruits and ice-cream will have a more delicate flavour if you add a few geranium leaves, fresh or dried.

Geranium leaves can also be used for infusions: crush a few leaves, place them in a pot and pour boiling water over them.

Geranium flowers are also edible, and can be used to decorate cakes.

Goose

When choosing a goose, make sure that the feet and bill are yellow; this means it will be young. When the bird is young, the feet are pliable; when old, the feet and bill are red.

See also *Poultry* on page 43.

Gooseberries

Use a pair of scissors to top and tail gooseberries.

Grapes

To keep grapes fresh for months, use bunches which have fully ripened and which are not too tight: remove any bad grapes. In a barrel or wooden box (in preference to plastic or cardboard) lay a coating of very dry bran. Place bunches of grapes on top and cover them with bran, then another layer of grapes and another layer of bran until the barrel or box is full. Close it and keep in a dry, coolish place. When you want grapes in the winter, just dip into the bran.

To freeze grapes, wash the grapes, remove from the stalks and dry them. Place them in a container and freeze. Serve them on a pretty dish after dinner with coffee; they are refreshing and taste like sorbet. The seedless variety is especially delicious.

Gratin

To prevent an unpleasant crust forming on the top of a dish au gratin in the oven or under the grill, mix the grated cheese with breadcrumbs, sprinkle with a little water and dot with butter. After a few minutes, take out the dish, sprinkle with a little water and finish browning.

Green and red peppers

To peel peppers, put them in a hot oven for 5 to 10 minutes, turning from time to time; this will loosen the skin. You can also char the skin over the gas burner of your cooker.

Greens

Many greens and herbs (e.g. mint, parsley, celery and lettuce) will keep fresh and crisp for a week if wrapped in a wet cloth. Keep the cloth wet, and store in the refrigerator or a cool place.

Hamburgers

A hamburger is cooked when small beads of blood begin to ooze through the crust.

Heating up a complete dinner in one pan

In a large pan place three or four jam jars containing stew, fish, rice, etc. Cover each jar with foil, and pour boiling water in the pan to come two-thirds of the way up the sides of the jars. Potatoes can be boiled in the water, and in this way a whole meal can be re-heated over one gas or electric ring.

Herbs

Dry herbs have a much stronger flavour than fresh ones. Half a teaspoon of dried, or $\frac{1}{4}$ teaspoon of powdered, is the equivalent of 2 level teaspoons of fresh herbs.

To freeze herbs, put the leaves in an ice-cube tray, pour water over, and freeze. When needed, take out one or two cubes, melt the ice and use the herbs as usual.

Never use metal containers for storing herbs as these can easily affect the delicate flavours. Use porcelain, earthenware, china or dark glass containers. The flavour and colour of herbs are affected by the daylight when kept in a transparent jar.

Herbs and garlic lose their flavour when over-cooked, so add them towards the end of the cooking time.

Herbal infusion

Fresh herbs: use 3 teaspoons of fresh bruised leaves for each cup. Bruise the leaves by crushing them in a clean linen cloth before use.

Dried herbs: use 1 teaspoon of herbs for each cup and one for the teapot.

Honey

If honey goes sugary, stand the jar in hot water and it will liquefy again.

Ice-cube trays

These are very useful for freezing liquids such as fruit juice, bouillon, stock and tomato sauce. When the liquid is frozen, transfer the cubes to plastic bags. Fruit juices should have a little sugar mixed into them before freezing (except for redcurrant juice, which would become jelly).

Jam and jelly

When making syrup for jam, do not stir the sugar and water once they start cooking or the sugar will crystallise.

If jam crystallises it is due to a lack of acid. To remedy, re-heat the jam with a little lemon juice.

If fur forms on the surface, jam is still good to eat. Carefully remove the mould and use the jam as soon as possible.

Lemon juice added to jam or jelly at the boiling stage will help the jam to set and improves the flavour.

Kippers

When dry, stand them in boiling water for 3 minutes, drain, dot with butter, and grill gently for 5 to 6 minutes.

Put the kippers in an earthenware pan, cover them with boiling water, put a lid on the pan and leave them for 7 to 10 minutes. They will swell a little and be cooked perfectly.

Lamb

In good-quality lamb the lean should be pale pink and fine-grained; the fat should be white and firm.

To test lamb, prick it with a skewer. If a colourless juice runs out, the meat is cooked.

See also *Meat* on page 35.

Lemons

Fresh lemon or orange juice frozen in ice-cube trays makes an original touch when mixing drinks.

To keep lemons fresh, store them in the refrigerator, or in a bowl of cold water, changing the water frequently. They will stay fresh and juicy for weeks.

Slices of lemon are difficult to squeeze. If lemon juice is needed for a dish, cut the lemon in wedges.

Frozen lemons are easier and quicker to grate than fresh ones.

A little lemon juice in a fruit salad helps to keep pear or apple slices from discolouring.

Grated lemon peel added to mincemeat improves the flavour.

Liver

Before cooking liver, soak it for an hour in milk. Dry it before cooking. The soaking will make the liver more tender and succulent.

Do not store liver in its wrapping or it will become dry and will stick to the paper. Brush some oil on the slices and wrap in aluminium foil or put on a covered plate before placing in the refrigerator.

Lobsters

The best lobsters are male, which are usually the smallest but do have the best flavour. When boiled, their colour is a deeper red than that of hen lobsters, which are better for sauces. The male lobster can be distinguished from the hen by the narrow back-part of the tail. The two uppermost fins within this section are stiff and hard, whereas those on the hen are soft and the tail is larger.

When buying lobsters, choose the heaviest ones. When lobsters are fresh, the claws will move slightly if you press the eyes with your fingers. When buying them ready-boiled, check whether the tails are stiff: if they are, the lobsters are fresh; if the tails are flabby, don't buy the lobsters.

Marigolds

Marigold petals can be used instead of saffron to colour food. They also have a light, delicate flavour. The petals can be used fresh or dried. Dry them in a cool, dark place in thin layers and they will retain their beautiful colour.

Mayonnaise

When mayonnaise curdles, pour a tablespoon of hot water into a bowl and then slowly pour the mayonnaise into it, stirring constantly until you achieve the right consistency. Add another tablespoon of hot water to stabilise the mixture.

Mustard helps mayonnaise to stabilise, as do a few drops of lemon juice.

When mayonnaise is ready, incorporate the beaten white of an egg; this will make it light and more digestible.

Meat

To keep raw meat fresh in hot weather when travelling, wash the meat with weak vinegar and water, then spread the meat with slices of raw onion. In this way it will keep perfectly fresh in the hottest weather. Before cooking, remove the onion and rinse the meat until no trace of onion remains. This method is also excellent for fowl (a raw onion placed inside the bird will prevent any musty flavour).

To prevent meat juices escaping, sear the surface of the meat quickly, then finish cooking at a low temperature. Cooking at a high temperature hardens the fibres and toughens meat.

Do not season the meat either before or during cooking as the salt makes the juices flow. Season at the end of the process.

A tough piece of meat will become tender if you marinate it overnight in beer before cooking. Any meat, including poultry, will improve if cooked in beer.

When thawing meat *do not* put the meat under a hot tap to thaw it more quickly, as this will make it tough.

Never keep meat stock overnight in copper, brass, tin or iron vessels as it could acquire an unpleasant flavour.

When roasting, do not add water to the meat or it will become tough. The meat should stand on a grill to avoid contact with the fat and juices.

To test white meat, prick it with a knife tip. If the juice runs clear and not pink, the meat is cooked. To test red meat, prick it with a fine skewer. If a light pink juice runs out, the meat is cooked.

When cooking meat, use tongs rather than a fork to turn it. Stabbing with a fork punches holes in the meat which allow the juices and therefore the flavour to drip out.

Minced meat should be eaten straight after being minced, or as soon as possible. Mince your own meat when needed; it does not take long and is well worth the effort. Do not mince it too finely.

See also under individual names.

Melons

Always wrap melon carefully before putting it in the refrigerator or its smell will spread and spoil other food.

A ripe melon should be slightly soft at the top when pressed gently. It should be heavy and have a good strong smell.

Melon with port, or seasoned with salt and freshly ground pepper, is delicious.

Meringues

For a soft consistency, the quantity of sugar must not exceed 1 oz (about 30 g) for each egg white. Any more will result in hard meringues.

Do not remove the meringues from the oven as soon as you turn it off. The longer they are left in, the better the result.

Milk

A wooden spoon standing in the saucepan will prevent milk, or custard, boiling over.

Never add milk to the tea in a thermos flask as it could curdle if left for any length of time.

Mint

To keep mint green when dry, first wash it in water to which bicarbonate of soda has been added: 2 level tablespoons of bicarbonate of soda to ½ pint (300 ml) of water.

To preserve mint for sauce, pick the mint when dry, choosing the most tender leaves. After chopping it finely, put in a jar. Do not press the mint down tightly or it will spoil the colour. Fill the jar with cold boiled vinegar, cover with a lid and leave. When you need mint sauce, take out a few spoonfuls and add sugar and vinegar to taste. Using this method, the mint will keep for months.

Mushrooms

When cleaning mushrooms, do not peel them as the skin has a very good flavour. Trim the sandy part and put the mushrooms in cold water with a few drops of vinegar (this will bring out any little insects hidden in the head). Wipe gently and then rapidly wash again twice. Dry carefully in a teatowel.

Muslin bags

When you have a little spare time, make a few muslin bags of different sizes. You will find them very convenient when you are using herbs in dishes where only the flavour is required.

Mussels

When buying mussels, do not choose ones with the shell open.

Do not eat any mussels which are still closed at the end of the cooking process, as they could be bad.

Mustard

A crushed clove of garlic added to mustard is very tasty.

To obtain the full flavour of mustard, mix the powder with salad oil, not water.

Mutton

In good-quality mutton, the lean should be dark red and fine-grained; the fat should be creamy-coloured and firm.

See also *Meat* on page 35.

Oil

Some oils are refined for consumption and others are not. The unrefined oils include olive oil, sunflower oil, corn oil, groundnut (peanut) oil, sesame oil and walnut oil. Ideally these have been cool-pressed, and have undergone very little more in the way of processing. Those oils that are refined have free fatty acids removed as well as particles of seed and juice. They lose some vitamins and minerals in the process, but their tendency to go rancid is reduced. Refined oils are useful for frying, but are a poor substitute for unrefined oils in dishes where the flavour of the oil is important.

Polyunsaturated oils have a high calorie content and provide energy. They also contain fatty acids essential to our diet. They can reduce blood cholesterol levels and so lessen the risk of coronary disease. The best polyunsaturated oils are cold-pressed (extra virgin) olive oil, sunflower oil, soya bean oil, safflower oil, groundnut oil and corn oil.

The best olive oil is cold-pressed oil that has not been heated or rectified. Its flavour is excellent; it is very pure, and contains many vitamins and minerals which are removed by heating and rectifying. It is expensive, and thus best kept for dishes where its distinctive flavour is important.

Sunflower and corn oils are very good for salad dressing and mayonnaise. They have no appreciable flavour. Sunflower oil is also a very good cooking oil.

Soya bean oil can only be used cold (e.g. for salads and mayonnaise). It takes on an unpleasant flavour at high temperatures, but it is much cheaper than other oils used for both frying and seasoning.

Groundnut oil is the best oil for frying as it will heat to a temperature of 390°F (200°C). Strain often and keep it in a dark container.

Make your own mock olive oil by filling up a quarter of a bottle with plain green olives. Pour over them a light, tasteless vegetable oil to fill the bottle, and then cork it. After two or three days your oil will have a delicious light olive flavour, lighter on the digestion than the real thing.

Omelettes

Two eggs for each person is the quantity usually required.

Slow cooking and over-cooking make the eggs tough, so never make an omelette with more than 8 eggs. A few little omelettes are tastier than one big one.

A dash of soda water in the beaten eggs will make the omelette much lighter.

Increase the volume by adding 1 tablespoon of milk or water for each egg used.

A few strokes with the fork will be enough to mix the eggs. Too much beating liquefies the eggs, which means that they will not swell when poured into the hot butter and the omelette will become heavy and not so tasty. If the eggs are beaten too far in advance they will take on a brownish colour.

Onions

Peel onions under running water. In this way they will not irritate the eyes and will not leave any smell on knife or hands.

Put onions in the freezer for 15 minutes before peeling. It fixes the volatile oil which would otherwise escape and which is the substance causing tears.

If the root end is held over a flame for a few moments or singed with a hot iron, the onion will not sprout when stored.

To peel small onions, immerse them in boiling water for 1 minute beforehand.

To remove the smell of onion from a wooden chopping board, rub it with salt.

Oranges

If you put an orange in the oven for a few minutes before peeling, the white fibres will come away easily with the rind.

Oven

When an electric oven is switched off it retains the heat for at least 20 minutes. So, to save fuel, switch it off before foods such as biscuits, small cakes and meringues are completely cooked.

Pancakes

When making pancakes, use only the yolk of an egg to begin with. If you add the lightly beaten white at the end, when the batter is ready for use, the pancakes will be much lighter.

Batter should be the consistency of thin cream, the thinner the better for light pancakes.

Half a pint of batter (300 ml) will make 7 to 8 pancakes.

To keep your pancakes warm while you are making others, put them one on top of the other on a plate which has been placed over a pan of boiling water, and cover the pancakes with a teatowel.

To re-heat pancakes, overlap them on a buttered baking sheet, brushing them lightly with melted butter as you do so. Place in a warm oven for about 15 to 30 minutes, until hot enough to serve. They taste exactly like freshly made pancakes even if they have been made the day before.

Pancakes can be frozen. For quick thawing, interleave them with greaseproof paper before freezing. To re-heat pancakes once thawed, wrap them in foil and place in a moderate oven for about 30 minutes.

Parsley

Parsley contains a lot of calcium and Vitamin C. Do use plenty of it – it stimulates the appetite and aids digestion.

To keep parsley, chop it finely and work it into butter. Store in the freezer – the butter will thaw very quickly when needed.

Scissors are useful for chopping parsley into a cup.

Pasta

To cook spaghetti, noodles and other pasta in an economical way, throw the pasta into boiling water and allow to come to the boil again. Turn off the heat and cover the pan with a thin teatowel and then the lid; leave for 15 minutes. The pasta will be cooked, will not stick and will never be over-cooked.

To stop pasta boiling over, put a few drops of oil in the water, or leave a wooden spoon standing in the saucepan during cooking.

To re-heat left-over pasta, dip it for a few seconds in boiling water. Drain and serve immediately.

Peaches

To peel peaches, immerse them in boiling water for a few seconds, then dip into cold water and the skin should come off easily.

Peanuts

Peanuts have a high protein content, and a large amount of minerals and B-complex vitamins which are necessary for growth and tissue building. They have a high calorie content and are very good for children's snacks.

Pepper

Pepper will stay dry in a wooden container, as the wood absorbs dampness.

Pies

If your pie does not brown nicely on top, a little sugar and water mixed together and brushed lightly on the crust will brown quickly when the pie is put back in the oven. It should be watched carefully at this stage.

Pineapple

A fresh, ripe pineapple should be heavy and have a strong sweet smell. Its scales should be reddish yellow, plump and shiny. When pulled, the leaves from the tuft should come off easily. A pineapple with brown spots is over-ripe.

Pineapple helps the digestion and is recommended after a rich dinner. It also acts as a laxative.

A pinch of salt sprinkled on fresh pineapple will neutralise the acidity of the fruit.

Pork

In good-quality pork the flesh should be lean and pink with a fine grain; the rind should be thin and smooth, and firm to the touch; the fat should be white and firm.

Cook pork slowly at first. Near the end of the cooking time, finish off quickly at a higher temperature to make the crackling crisp.

To test pork, prick it with a skewer. If a colourless juice runs out, the meat is cooked.

Pork cutlets will be tastier if, before frying or grilling, you soak them in boiling water for 2 or 3 minutes.

See also *Meat* on page 35.

Potatoes

Baked potatoes retain virtually all their Vitamin C, whereas more than two-thirds is lost if they are peeled and boiled. You lose less by boiling them in their skins.

Germinating potatoes provoke the birth and development of toxic alkaloids which are harmful to health. Always cut off the germinating part before cooking the potatoes.

Before baking potatoes, stand them in hot water for 15 minutes. The cooking time will be halved and the potatoes will be mealy and more tasty.

For a crisp skin on baked potatoes, rub with a little butter or oil and sprinkle with salt before baking. If you push a skewer through the potato it will conduct the heat to the centre and help it to cook much more quickly.

Old potatoes will taste as good as new if, before cooking, you stand them for 2 or 3 hours in cold water. Then plunge them into boiling salted water. When cooked, pour off the water and put the pan of potatoes back on a low heat for 5 minutes, shaking from time to time.

When boiling peeled old potatoes, add a few drops of vinegar to the water near the end of the cooking time to prevent the flesh becoming dark.

Mashed potatoes

The best mashed potatoes in the world (a little extravagant but ...) are cooked in milk. When the potatoes are cooked, discard the milk (or give it to the cat) and mash the potatoes with butter.

For deliciously light mashed potatoes, add the yolk of an egg and, at the last minute, the stiffly beaten white. A touch of garlic also makes a pleasant change.

Poultry

When you are buying poultry for roasting, the breast-bone should be elastic and crisp, the breast plump, the neck and legs fat. The skin should be white and clear.

Old birds for boiling should have a plump appearance, clear skin and a firm breast-bone.

Before cooking older birds, the sinews (pieces of tough, fibrous tissue uniting the muscles and the bone) should be removed; this will relax the muscles and make the meat tender. To remove the sinews, take a sharp knife and make a slit in the leg above the claw to reveal the sinews. Draw out each sinew from the flesh, using a skewer slipped under the sinew and holding the foot tightly as you pull.

If you have a tough bird, soak it in cold water overnight before boiling and it will be beautifully tender.

To test poultry, prick with a skewer. If a colourless juice runs out, the bird is cooked.

See also under individual names.

Prawns or shrimps

To moisten dry prawns or shrimps, soak them in milk before cooking.

Puddings

When baking milk puddings, custards, etc. in the oven, place the dish in a tin of water to prevent the pudding burning.

Rabbit and hare

When fresh, these have smooth, sharp claws, bright eyes, and unbroken ears that are smooth, tender and easily torn.

Radishes

It is easy to make pretty radish flowers. Trim off the root end and leaves of the radish and cut lengthwise six or eight times without

severing the base. Put the cut radishes into a bowl of cold water in the refrigerator and leave them to stand for an hour or so. The sections will open up and curl like a flower. This can also be done with celery: cut the sticks (3 inches, 6 cm long) into fine strips to within 1 inch (2 cm) of one end and put in cold water for a while.

Raisins

To stone raisins, pour boiling water over them and leave for a few minutes before draining. Rub each raisin between the thumb and finger to bring out the seeds. Dry the raisins before use.

Redcurrants

Use a fork to strip redcurrants from their stalks.

Rhubarb

Do not eat rhubarb leaves – they are poisonous.

Before cooking rhubarb, cut it up and soak it for 45 minutes in cold water with a teaspoon of bicarbonate of soda. The water will become dark, which means that the acidity has been drawn out. Less sugar will be needed, too.

Rice

One cup of raw rice yields 3 cups of cooked rice.

A teaspoon or two of lemon juice in the cooking water helps to keep the rice white and the grains separate. A few drops of oil in the boiling water will also keep the grains separate.

Rusks

To butter rusks, French *biscottes* and other crumbly biscuits without breaking them, stack them in a pile, butter the top one and put it at the bottom of the pile. Repeat until all the biscuits are buttered; none will break.

Salads

Fresh lettuces straight from the garden or grower will keep for over a week if wrapped in newspaper and stored in a dark, cool corner before being washed or trimmed.

Lettuce should be washed by dunking it up and down, head first, in a container of cold water. The suction draws out the dirt. To prevent the leaves going brown, they should be separated carefully by pulling them apart and tearing them with the fingers, *not* cutting them with a knife.

For a very crisp green salad, pour the dressing into the salad bowl and set aside. After washing and draining the salad, put it in a plastic bag in the refrigerator for at least half an hour before it is required and it will be lovely and crisp. Don't wash salad that you want to store in the refrigerator.

When mixing salad always use a large bowl; it is then much easier to toss the leaves.

For potato salad with oil and vinegar, the potatoes must be dressed while still hot.

For potato salad with mayonnaise, the potatoes must be dressed when cold.

Salad dressing

Make up a quantity of oil and vinegar dressing in a jar so that it can be stored in the refrigerator for a week to 10 days. The dressing has a better flavour this way, and is ready when you need it.

Use corn oil or olive oil and wine vinegar (this has a more delicate flavour than malt vinegar), a teaspoon of mustard and a pinch of sugar to give the dressing a pleasant bite.

If you don't like garlic in your salad, try a grated onion – it gives a delicious flavour. If you do like garlic in your salad but do not like pieces of it, rub the inside of the salad bowl with a cut clove of garlic.

Salt

Salt stays dry in wooden and porous stoneware containers as they absorb dampness.

To prevent salt from becoming damp, put a piece of blotting paper at the bottom of its container. A few grains of rice mixed with the salt will also stop it becoming damp.

A pinch of salt in the frying pan before putting butter, oil or other fat to melt will prevent any splashing during cooking.

Coarse salt or sea salt ground in a salt mill will give a better flavour to food.

To extract water from vegetables such as cucumber or tomatoes before adding them to a salad, sprinkle them with a little salt after slicing and leave for 15 minutes. Drain off the liquid before putting the vegetables into the salad.

Salty food

A raw potato added to a soup or stew that has become too salty will take much of the saltiness away.

Sandwiches

When making sandwiches containing mustard, mix the mustard and butter together before spreading. The mustard will be evenly distributed and the sandwich making will be much quicker.

Put mayonnaise between two lettuce leaves in a sandwich so that it will not soak into the bread if the sandwich is left to stand.

Sauces

If your white sauce has become lumpy, pour it in a jar or plastic bottle, put the lid on tightly and shake vigorously. The lumps will disappear and the sauce will become smooth. Alternatively, you can sieve the sauce or, if you have an electric blender, you can blend the sauce for a few seconds.

A large clean marble put into a sauce or stew after it has been thickened will stir the sauce and also stop it burning.

Sausage

Prick the skin before cooking to prevent the sausage from bursting.

Saving electricity or gas

Use a plate made of a heat-conducting metal, big enough to hold two saucepans. Put this on the ring of your cooker and you will be able to cook two dishes for the price of one.

Scissors

Scissors are useful for snipping dried fruit or peel (for cakes, puddings or mincemeat) instead of chopping them.

Use scissors for cutting fresh herbs, removing stalks and veins from cabbage leaves, and cutting off cress roots and radish leaves.

Scissors can also be used to cut meat for stews, or to trim fish.

Shellfish

Shellfish which is to be eaten cold should always be left to cool off in the court bouillon in which it was cooked. Drain only when completely cold.

Soufflés

Small soufflés are easier to make than large ones, so use two dishes instead of one. Fill the dishes no more than three-quarters full. Start the cooking on a hotplate for 2 minutes and warm the dish first. If the mixture is already warm, a salted soufflé will cook much more quickly.

Spinach

Spinach shrinks when cooking. To obtain 1 lb (about 500 g) of cooked spinach you will need about 3 lb (about 1½ kg) of raw spinach.

Spinach cooked without water retains much more flavour and

goodness. To prepare it, wash and drain the spinach, put it in a saucepan over a low heat and turn often. Enough moisture will soon appear to cook it.

Stews

To rescue a stew which is burning, dip the pan quickly into cold water. The effect of the cold water will make the stew leave the bottom of the pan. Turn into another pan and continue cooking, adding more liquid if necessary.

Strawberries

Wash strawberries *before* hulling them, or they will absorb the water.

Sugar

If you do not have icing sugar you can make some by crushing granulated or caster sugar in an electric blender.

Sweets

To stop sweets sticking together, sprinkle them with powdered sugar.

Syrup or treacle

To weigh golden syrup or treacle, flour the scales well and then pour in the syrup. You will find it will leave the scales easily. The same applies if you are measuring with spoons.

Tarts

To avoid soggy pastry in fruit tarts, sprinkle the bottom and sides of the pastry case with a mixture of flour and sugar before putting in the fruit. This only applies to tarts which are to be cooked.

Thickening

To thicken a soup, mix 1 tablespoon of flour or arrowroot with a walnut-sized piece of butter and 3 tablespoons of the soup. Mix well, then pour into the soup, stirring constantly until the butter is melted. Cook for 5 minutes without boiling.

Thyme

Use thyme to aid the digestion of fatty food, especially pork and mutton.

Tomatoes

Tomatoes are acid. A pinch of sugar in your tomato sauce will improve the taste.

Tomato paste

Left-over tomato paste will keep perfectly in the refrigerator if you coat it with a thin layer of oil.

Turkey

After cooking a turkey, take it out of the oven at least 45 minutes before carving. Keep it in a warm place, covered with a warm cloth. This will allow the fibres to settle and the turkey will be more tender.

See also *Poultry* on page 43.

Veal

This is looser in texture than any other meat. The best veal should have pale pink flesh which is dry to the touch, and white fat which is firm and fairly transparent.

To test veal, prick it with a skewer. If a colourless juice runs out, the meat is cooked.

See also *Meat* on page 35.

Vegetables

Most of the nutritive value of vegetables is in the outer leaves or just under the skin, so the mineral salts can easily be lost if the vegetables are carelessly prepared. Where possible, cook vegetables in their skin; if you must peel them, do so thinly.

When washing fresh vegetables, do not leave them too long in the water as this dilutes the mineral salts. For the same reason, never cut them into small pieces.

To cook several vegetables separately in one pan of water, pack each one (carrots, string beans, cabbage, etc.) in foil. Take account of the different cooking times: put the ones which need most cooking in first, and then those that cook more quickly, so that they are ready together. Each vegetable will retain its flavour, and you will save fuel.

Never throw away the water in which your vegetables have been cooked. Use it for making gravy, soups, etc.

Green vegetables cooked in copper utensils keep their colour better, as copper has properties which preserve the chlorophyll.

Vinegar

To strengthen vinegar, freeze it repeatedly and remove the ice from the surface.

Herb vinegar can easily be made at home by putting fresh sprigs of your favourite herbs in a bottle of vinegar.

Vodka

Vodka should be drunk very cold. The best place to keep it is in the freezer, and the best way to serve it is to have the bottle wrapped in a block of ice. This effect is easy to achieve: before putting the bottle of vodka in the freezer, place it in a cylindrical container long enough and large enough for the bottle with at least 1½ inches (3 cm) of space all around. Fill the container with water three-quarters of the way up the bottle, and place in the freezer. When you need it, run warm water over the container – the bottle, in its block of ice, will slide out easily. A pretty touch can be added if half-way through freezing, when the water around the bottle is still at the icicle stage, you slide some flowers or leaves into it.

To flavour vodka with lemon, place the skin of half a lemon in the bottle of vodka and leave to macerate for 24 hours. Strain before use.

To flavour vodka with red pepper, place 1 red pepper in the bottle of vodka and leave to macerate for 1 hour only before straining.

Walnuts

To peel walnuts that are very dry, soak them in water for a few hours beforehand. This will soften them and prevent them breaking as they are peeled.

Watercress

Watercress should be thoroughly washed before being eaten as it often grows in water where it can be contaminated by animals.

Watermelons

To have fresh melons all year round, buy them when they are sweet and juicy and coat them thoroughly with plaster of Paris or, better still, plaster of Paris bandages (obtainable from chemists). Store in a cool dark place. When you want to use one, break the plaster cast and you will find the melon is as fresh as if newly bought. Try this method with other varieties of melon, too.

Waxed paper

Put sheets of waxed paper between pieces of meat and fish fillets before freezing. The parcels will then separate easily.

Wine

Never store bottled wine upright, as the cork will become dry and the wine might become tainted. Bottles should be stored on their side.

Wooden salad bowls

After use, rinse wooden salad bowls in cold water only. From time to time, clean with warm oil and dry with a paper towel.

Use wooden forks and spoons for mixing a salad, as these do not bruise the leaves.

Yeast

If frozen, yeast will stay effective and in good condition for at least 3 months. Before freezing, cut it in small pieces of 1oz (about 30g) which is the usual amount required for bread making. Wrap in foil and place in a labelled and dated plastic bag. Thawing can be hastened by placing the yeast in cold water.

Yogurt

Yogurt does not freeze well as it separates when frozen, although this can sometimes be corrected by whisking. Sweetened fruit yogurt does freeze quite well.

People with delicate digestions find yogurt easier to digest than milk.

Storing food

In the cupboard

These foods should be stored in airtight containers in a cool, dry place. The storage times given below are the minimum: some food may last longer and might still be edible after a few years. The times refer to unopened packages.

Cereals	Oatmeal (Its high fat content can cause it to become rancid, so do not store for too long.)	Up to 2 months
	Breakfast cereals	Buy in small amounts

Coffee	Vacuum-packed	1 year
	Ground, gas-packed	3 months
	Unground, gas-packed	6 months
	Instant	3–5 months
Cornflour		Up to 1 year
Custard powder		Up to 3 months
Dried fruits	Need dry, cool storage. They can shrink if kept too warm, or ferment if too damp.	6 months to 1 year
Dried herbs, spices, seasonings		6 months
Flavourings		Indefinitely
Flour	Flour and semolina keep well in suitable conditions, but can be affected by insects, so be watchful and throw away any that becomes contaminated. Check in case the damage has spread.	
	Self-raising	Up to 2 years
	Plain white	Up to 2 years
	Wholemeal (Its high fat content can turn it rancid. Do not store too long.)	Up to 3 months
Fruit	In glass	4–6 months
Fruit drinks	In glass	1 year
	In plastic	4–6 months
Mayonnaise (bought)		6–8 months
Mint sauce		1 year
Nuts	Their fat content can cause them to become rancid.	
	Almonds	
	Coconut (shredded)	Buy in small
	Peanuts	amounts
	Walnuts	

Oil	Olive or other cooking oil, in glass or plastic	1 year
Pasta		2–3 years
Pickles		2 years
Pulses	Beans Dried peas Lentils	1–2 years
Rice	Ground rice Semolina Tapioca	1–2 years
Salad cream		6–8 months
Sauces	Bottled, unopened	2 years
Sugar	Brown Caster Granulated Icing	Up to 3 years
	Demerara goes lumpy if kept for too long.	Buy small amounts
Syrups	Golden syrup Treacle	1–2 years
Tea	Tea bags Packet tea	6 months 4–6 months

Tins   Tinned food should be stored in a cool, dry place. When kept too long, tinned food first loses most of its colour, and then its flavour and smell. If the top of a tin is no longer flat, but raised, the tin should be discarded as it means that the food is fermenting inside (unless it is a fizzy drink, beer or ground coffee). Leaky tins are usually caused by rust and should not be used as the food inside has probably been contaminated. Food should never be stored in an opened tin: transfer it to another container.

Fish (sardines, mackerel, pilchards, herrings, etc.) in brine	3 years
Fish, in tomato sauce	1 year
Fruits (soft, stoned)	1 year
Fruit juice	6–9 months
Honey and jam	2 years

	Meat, ham	2–3 years
	Milk (dried) will keep well although it might lose some of its flavour after 3 months.	3 years
	Milk (sweetened, condensed)	6–10 months
	Pasta, in tomato sauce	8–12 months
	Soup	1–2 years
	Tomato purée	1 year
	Vegetables (baked beans, broad beans, carrots, etc.)	Up to 2 years
Vegetables	In glass	4–6 months
Vinegar		3 years

In the refrigerator

Cheese	In original pack or foil	1–3 weeks
	Cream cheese in covered container or foil	1 week
Eggs	Hard-boiled, in shell	5–6 days
	Yolks, covered with water	2 days
	Whites, separated, in covered container	2 days
Fish	Raw, loosely covered in foil	1–2 days
	Cooked, loosely covered in foil or in a covered container	1–2 days
Fruits	Stone and hard fruits, lightly wrapped	4–8 days
	Soft fruits, cleaned, in covered container or in the crisper	2–3 days
Meat, raw		
Chops	Rinse under clear water,	3–4 days
Roasts	wipe dry, wrap loosely in	3–5 days
Steaks	foil and refrigerate	3–4 days
Stewing	straight away.	2–3 days
Offal		1 day
Bacon		8–10 days
Smoked ham		1 week

Meat, cooked	Joints, in a covered container or wrapped in foil	4–5 days
	Casseroles	2–3 days
Milk	Fresh, in bottle or covered container	4 days
	Cultured, in original container	8–10 days
	Custard, milk sweets, in covered dishes	2 days
Poultry, raw	Washed, dried, wrapped in aluminium foil	2–3 days
Poultry, cooked	Refrigerated as soon as cool (stuffing removed), wrapped in foil.	3–4 days
	Dishes, cooled and refrigerated in covered container	1–2 days
Vegetables	Greens, loosely wrapped or in crisper	4–5 days
	Salad, loosely wrapped or in crisper	4–7 days

Servings

Servings, of course, vary with appetite, but on average the following quantities are sufficient for one person. Weights are for uncooked food. (Metric equivalents are approximate only.)

Fish	Headless, cleaned and skinned, with bones	8 oz (250 g)
	Whole, with head, bones, skin and tail	1 lb (500 g)
	Fillets	6 oz (200 g)
	Steaks, with bone and skin	7 oz (220 g)
	Smoked, with bones	8 oz (250 g)
	Smoked, filleted	6 oz (200 g)
Game	Hare	10 oz (300 g)
	Rabbit	10 oz (300 g)
	Venison	8 oz (250 g)
	Grouse	1 portion
	Partridge (young)	1–1½ portions
	Pheasant	3 portions
	Pigeon	1 portion
	Quail	1 portion
	Snipe	1 portion
	Woodcock	1 portion
Meat	Beef, pork, veal, with bone	8 oz (250 g)
	Beef, pork, veal, without bone	6 oz (200 g)
	Minced meat	6 oz (200 g)
Poultry, on the bone	Chicken, roast	10 oz (300 g)
	Chicken, boiling	14 oz (450 g)
	Poussin, one small bird	1 portion
	Duck	1 lb (500 g)
	Goose	1 lb (500 g)
	Guinea fowl	12 oz (400 g)
	Turkey	14 oz (450 g)

(For the Game section, Grouse, Partridge, Pheasant, Pigeon, Quail, Snipe and Woodcock are marked "One bird".)

Pulses, Rice, Pasta	Beans	2 oz (60 g)
	Lentils	2 oz (60 g)
	Pasta	3 oz (90 g)
	Peas	2 oz (60 g)
	Rice	2½ oz (75 g)
Shellfish	Crab, in shell	12 oz (400 g)
	Lobster, in shell	8 oz (250 g)
	Scallops (depending on dish served)	1 or 2 per portion
	Oysters, fresh, as starter	at least 6 per portion
	Mussels	¾ pint (450 ml)
	Shrimps, peeled	4 oz (120 g)
Vegetables	Asparagus	12 oz (400 g)
	Cabbage	6–8 oz (200–250 g)
	Carrots, old	8 oz (250 g)
	Carrots, new	6 oz (200 g)
	Green beans	10 oz (300 g)
	Peas, in pod	8 oz (250 g)
	Potatoes, old	1 lb (500 g)
	Potatoes, new	8 oz (250 g)
	Spinach	1 lb (500 g)

Household

Cleaning agents

The following are the basic cleaning agents needed in a household and referred to throughout this chapter.

Ammonia

Gives off strong fumes, so use in a well-ventilated room and wear rubber gloves. Keep in a cool, dark place. It removes stains such as grease, chocolate and blood from fabrics. For household purposes use 10 per cent solution in water.

Bicarbonate of soda

Useful for removing acid stains (e.g. fruit) from fabrics, and for softening water to be used for cooking.

Glycerine

A colourless, odourless liquid which is a useful solvent for removing stains from washable fabrics (fruit, coffee, etc.). Glycerine dissolves in warm water, but not in cleaning fluid. Do not use it on non-washable fabrics.

Hydrogen peroxide

A colourless liquid used for bleaching. Keep in a cool, dark place. It is used for delicate treatments such as cleaning marble or ivory, and removing light scorch marks or stains such as blood, ink and perfume from fabrics.

Jeweller's rouge

An abrasive red powder. Use it as a paste mixed with methylated spirit or water. It is good for removing light scratches on glass or for polishing jewellery.

Linseed oil

Can be used to darken woods, especially oak. It will get rid of water marks on wood when mixed in equal proportions with turpentine.

Methylated spirit

Volatile and inflammable, this should be handled with care. It is a grease solvent good for cleaning mirrors, jewellery and ivory, and for removing grease stains from fabrics. It will also remove ballpoint or felt-tip ink stains, chocolate, coffee or mud stains from non-washable fabrics and old ink stains from carpets.

Paraffin

A colourless, odourless substance useful as a solvent for grease. It can be used as a substitute for beeswax.

Sandpaper

Use fine sandpaper for polishing rusty metal, also for cleaning suede shoes, suede collars, etc.

Turpentine

A good solvent for varnish, wax, paint, etc. It is quite expensive; white spirit will often be as effective and is much cheaper.

Vinegar

A mild acid, vinegar is a most useful cleaning agent around the house. Few other products have as many culinary and chemical virtues. It dissolves dirt deposits, and softens water (3 tablespoons to 1 pint, 600 ml). White vinegar will remove stains on fabric, carpets, etc. Hot vinegar will soften paint brushes.

Washing soda

This is a strong, very concentrated alkali, and can be injurious to the skin, so wear rubber gloves when using it. It clears grease from waste pipes, is used for cleaning silver and copper, and softens water for cleaning purposes.

White spirit

A good turpentine substitute. It is a solvent for paint, varnish and grease. It removes stains from fabric or carpets (e.g. paint, perfume) and from leather.

General hints

Alabaster

To clean alabaster, rub softly with a cloth dipped in turpentine or white spirit, which will clean and polish it at the same time.

To maintain alabaster, wax it every 6 months with a natural-colour wax and shine with a soft cloth.

Aluminium

Aluminium pans should not be used to boil the water for tea, as the metal gives the tea a disagreeable colour. Some foods (e.g. white soups or white sauces) will also become slightly discoloured if cooked in aluminium as it causes a small but harmless chemical reaction.

Do not wash aluminium pans in water mixed with washing soda, as this would damage the protective film on the aluminium which prevents corrosion.

To clean aluminium, use a piece of crumpled kitchen foil. When rubbed over the aluminium it restores a bright new look.

To clean aluminium utensils, rub them with a mixture of salad oil and methylated spirit. Use equal quantities of both and it will clean the aluminium perfectly.

Wood ash made into a paste with a little lemon juice or vinegar is also very good for cleaning and polishing aluminium. Use a wire pad dipped in wood ash to get rid of any brown stains.

To clean a burnt aluminium saucepan, fill with water, add an onion, and boil. The burn will soon loosen and come to the surface, leaving the pan clean and bright.

Stained aluminium cooking utensils which do not respond to the usual cleansing can be restored to brightness by cooking apples or apple peel in them. This does not affect the taste or do any harm to the apples.

Amber

To clean dirty amber, rub it gently with a piece of cottonwool dipped in methylated spirit and then polish it with a chamois leather.

To maintain clean amber, rub a little almond oil over it and polish with a chamois leather.

Ash

Cigarette or cigar ash can easily start a fire, so do not empty your ashtrays into a wastepaper basket. Use a large tin (coffee tins are good for this), empty your ashtrays into it and put the lid on tightly.

Ash can be used to remove heat marks on a polished table (see *Stains on wood* on page 110).

Bags

To remove water stains, hold your leather bag over a pan of boiling water for a little while. Wait until the leather is dry, then apply neutral polish.

Bamboo

To clean bamboo, wash it with a sponge or cloth soaked in warm soapy and salty water; use a soft brush if needed. Rinse and dry. Shine with a wax polish.

Barrels

To clean a barrel, wash thoroughly with a mixture of washing soda and boiling water (2 tablespoons of soda to 1 gallon or 4 litres of water) then rinse well.

Baths

If your bath (or basin) has stains caused by a dripping tap, rub the stains with a paste made of salt and lemon juice and then rinse. If the stains are old and resistant, make a paste of cream of tartar and peroxide. Rub the stain with a brush (an old toothbrush will do), rinse and hope for the best!

Beads

Children love threading beads, but often the limpness of the thread discourages them. Dip the end of the thread in nail varnish and leave it to dry, or rub it with soap. The thread will be stiff enough to pass through the beads easily.

Bleach

To get rid of the smell of bleach on your hands, rub with vinegar and then rinse.

Bone

See *Ivory and bone* on page 81.

Books

Pages can be repaired, if not too badly torn, with the white of an egg. Place the torn pieces in position and smear lightly with the egg white. Leave the book open to dry.

Surface dirt on book pages can be removed with fresh bread kneaded into a ball and rubbed gently over the paper.

Bottles

When packing bottles of liquid always stick a piece of adhesive plaster over the cork or stopper to prevent accidents, and always pack bottles in between soft items.

To clean bottles stained with vinegar, put some potato peelings into the bottle and fill with water. Allow to stand until the peelings ferment, then empty the bottle and wash. The glass should be crystal-clear.

See also *Decanters* on page 72.

Bran

Hot bran absorbs dirt and grease and freshens up fur or felt. Do not treat light-coloured felt with bran.

Brass

To clean brass, first wash in liquid detergent, then rub with a mixture of 1½ tablespoons of soap, 2½ tablespoons of vinegar and 1 pint (½ litre) of water.

To remove old polish from engraved brass, use an old toothbrush dipped in ammonia.

Brass and copper

To clean brass and copper, rub with a raw lemon dipped in a paste of powdered pumice and lemon juice, or a raw lemon dipped in fine salt.

To clean badly neglected copper and brass, take a container (not aluminium), put a good quantity of washing soda in it, add water, immerse the brass or copper piece in the solution, bring to the boil and simmer gently for an hour or more. (The solution of washing soda should be strong: 8 tablespoons of washing soda to 1 gallon or 4 litres of water.)

Bronze

To clean bronze, use soap and water applied with a soft brush. After rinsing, warm the bronze on a radiator and apply natural wax (liquid) with a paintbrush. Leave it to dry and then rub off any excess wax. When the bronze is cold, shine it with a soft cloth.

Brushes

To wash a bristle hairbrush, never use soap. Take a piece of soda, dissolve it in warm water and stand the brush in it so that the water covers only the bristles. It will become clean after a few minutes. To dry, stand the brush with the bristles pointing downwards.

Buttons

See *Sewing* on page 92.

Candles

To make candles last twice as long, hold them by the wick and coat with clear varnish. Leave to dry and harden: the varnish forms a hard coat which prevents the grease from running.

To prevent candles from dripping, soak them overnight in salted water; or sprinkle a little household salt around the top of the candle before lighting it.

To make candles fit the candlesticks, dip the ends in hot water until soft enough to be moulded to the required size.

Cane

To treat sagging cane seats on chairs, clean thoroughly on both sides with soap and hot water. Dry in the open air; this will cause the cane to shrink and often will make it as firm as new.

Baskets made of cane should be washed regularly in warm water. Cane is stronger and more supple when kept moist.

Carpets

For a method of preventing the edges of carpets curling up, see *Mats* on page 85.

Casting

To cut a piece of casting, first heat a handsaw until red-hot: the casting will cut like wood.

Chamois

To clean chamois when it is hard and dirty, soak in warm suds to which half a cup of cooking oil has been added. Soften well with your hands, and, unless the chamois is used for cleaning windows or mirrors, do not rinse or wring but press in a towel to dry (do not hang it outside). If the chamois is needed for cleaning windows and mirrors, rinse it before drying.

Chimney fires

If a chimney fire occurs, first shut all doors and windows. Seal the bottom of the chimney with a piece of wet blanket so that the draught is stopped; the burning soot will be extinguished for lack of air. If every fireplace were provided with a damper or shutter made of iron or tin plate, large enough to seal it thoroughly, chimney fires would not be such a problem.

Quickly put some wet newspaper on the fire and the steam will extinguish a chimney fire.

Throw about 1 lb (500 g) of washing soda, well dampened, on the fire and the fumes will extinquish the flames.

Chimneys

A cure for smoking chimneys is to fill a large ox-bladder with air and tie it by the neck to the middle of a stick placed across the inside of the chimney, about 3 feet (1 metre) from the top. The rising air keeps the bladder continually moving in a circular motion, which prevents a rush of air down the chimney.

China

To clean a crack in china where dust and grease have collected, bleach it with a cottonwool pad dipped in hydrogen peroxide and then rinse.

Badly stained coarse china can be cleaned by soaking in neat domestic bleach for a few days. Rinse well.

Chrome

To clean chrome, rub a soft cloth dampened in vinegar over it and polish dry with a clean soft cloth.

Cigarette burns

Burns on bakelite (plastic) can be removed by rubbing metal polish or paste on the marks.

Collars

A shiny coat collar can be cleaned by sponging it with a cloth or sponge moistened with vinegar or ammonia.

Copper

To clean any copper utensils dulled or blackened by fire, rub them with half a lemon dipped in salt. Wash them afterwards in water to prevent the acid corroding the copper.

To clean very dirty old copper, bring some bleach to the boil and dip the object in it. Remove it immediately as the bleach will strip metal left in it too long.

Tarnished copper equipment can be cleaned with a mixture made of $1/3$ flour, $1/3$ silver sand, $1/3$ fine salt, adding enough vinegar to make a paste. When the copper is cleaned, rinse thoroughly and dry.

See also *Brass and copper* on page 67.

Coral

Coral needs to be fed with a mixture of 1 tablespoon of turpentine or white spirit to 3 tablespoons of almond oil. Rub gently, then wipe with tissue paper and leave for one day before polishing with a chamois leather.

Corks

Cork swells, and sometimes a cork will not fit back into a bottle. Just drop it into boiling water for a minute or two; it will become soft and easy to fit back into the bottle.

Corkscrew

An improvised corkscrew can be made by attaching a piece of strong string to an ordinary screw.

Crockery

Use broken crockery to line plant pots.

Crocodile skin

To clean crocodile skin (handbags, shoes, belts, etc.) rub the skin gently with a little almond oil on a pad of cottonwool. Then polish with a soft cloth.

Cupboards

To keep a cupboard dry, fill a box with lime and place it on a shelf. This will absorb any dampness and also keep the air in the cupboard sweet.

Curtain rods

When threading a rod through the top hem of a curtain, a thimble placed on the end of the rod will allow it to run through smoothly without continually catching on the fabric.

Cutlery

After cleaning table cutlery, wash it in the usual way to prevent traces of the cleaning product contaminating your food.

Darning

Never darn with extra-thick thread to save time, as it will tear the fabric.

Decanters

To clean decanters and bottles, put small pieces of raw potato in them with equal parts of vinegar and water and shake for a few minutes.

To remove stains from a decanter, fill it with 1 pint (½ litre) of water in which you have mixed 5 tablespoons of domestic bleach. Rinse thoroughly.

To dry the insides of decanters (or bottles), use a hairdryer. Blow hot air into the decanter, keeping the hairdryer about 2 inches (4 cm) from the mouth. You can also dry them by warming them slightly and blowing air into them with a pair of bellows. If you don't have bellows, then a piece of rolled-up paper or a tube long enough to reach almost to the bottom of the decanter can be used; but *draw out* the damp air with the mouth, do not blow into the vessel.

Another way to dry decanters or bottles for display is to drain all the water out and then rinse with a tablespoon of methylated spirits. This will quickly evaporate, leaving the glass very clear. If you want to use the decanter later, rinse it with water.

Doors

A creaking door will be silenced at once if soap is applied to the hinges.

Drains

To clear drains, from time to time put a few lumps of washing soda on top of the grid and pour over boiling water.

Do not throw away coffee grounds: pour them down the kitchen sink to keep the drains free of grease.

Drawers

Soap or candle wax rubbed along the upper edges of tight-fitting drawers will make them run smoothly.

Dyeing

To dye a garment black successfully, use an equal quantity of navy-blue dye with the black dye. This will prevent the fabric taking on a greenish tinge.

Ebony

To renew the lustre of ebony when the blackness wears off leaving a brown surface, give it the following treatment. Wash with warm soapy water to remove any grease or dirt. Allow to dry and then apply the black dye used for suede shoes. When it is quite dry, polish with a good furniture cream and it will look as good as new.

Egg cartons

Plastic egg cartons make very successful paint boxes for children. Just put a little paint in each hole.

Elastic

Before drawing an old elastic or ribbon out of a hem to replace it, pin (with a small safety pin) or sew one end of the old piece to one end of the new one and pull the old elastic (or ribbon) out. This is a quick and simple method.

Embroidery

An easy way to copy embroidery from any material is to place a piece of paper over the embroidery and rub over it firmly with the back of a spoon. The design will appear on the paper very quickly.

Enamel

Do not use coarse cleaning powders on enamel surfaces, as they will scratch.

Stains can be removed by filling the enamel vessel with cold water to which 1 or 2 tablespoons of bleach are added. Leave to stand until the stains disappear and rinse well afterwards. To clean the outside of the pan, use a fine abrasive powder (pumice powder) and a strong detergent.

Fabric

Heavy fabric such as canvas will be easier to sew if the hems or seams are first rubbed with soap, thus enabling the needle to pass through the fabric more easily.

Felt

Use hot bran to clean felt. Heat the bran in the oven and then rub over the felt; it will absorb any grease. Brush thoroughly.

Fire lighters

Soak old newspapers or any unglazed paper for several days in a bucket of water, then tear up the pulp and squeeze it into hard balls. Place these in a warm place to dry and they will be excellent for lighting fires or for keeping fires burning.

Fires

A fire will burn better if there is a good bed of ashes to hold the heat.

To revive a dying fire, throw two or three handfuls of coarse salt on to it.

See also *Newspaper* on page 85.

Foam crumbs

When filling a cushion with foam crumbs, mix larger pieces of foam with the crumbs to prevent the pieces moving around when the cushion is sat on.

Funnel

A funnel is the perfect home for a ball of string. Hang the funnel on a hook in the kitchen, or wherever required, and draw the string through the funnel when needed.

Furniture

Do not leave varnished furniture exposed to sunlight: the wood becomes discoloured and it is impossible to restore its veneer.

Fur

To clean small pieces of fur, heat bran in the oven, rub it over the article and then brush thoroughly.

Fuses

When changing fuses, remember to turn off the electricity at the mains before touching the fuse box.

Keep a torch and a card of fuse wire near the fuse box in case of an emergency.

Label all fuses so that you know where they belong when one blows.

Gas

Make sure that you know where the main gas tap is, and how to use it, in case of emergency.

Gilt

To clean a gilt frame, use the water in which onions have been boiled, which will greatly improve its appearance.

Another method of cleaning gilt is to use 4 tablespoons of bleach mixed with 1 egg white: using a soft brush, clean the frame with this mixture and the gilt will brighten straight away. This procedure can be repeated until the gilt looks like new, after which the frame can be sealed with a special varnish to help it keep its appearance.

Glass

Light scratches on the surface of glass can be treated with a mixture of jeweller's rouge and a few drops of methylated spirit. Rub the paste gently over the scratches until they disappear, then wash and polish the glass with a soft cloth.

When clearing broken glass, you will find that any slivers remaining after the large pieces have been swept up can be collected by dabbing them with a damp tissue or paper napkin.

Glasses and jars

If drinking glasses stick together, place the bottom glass in hot water and fill up the top one with cold water. They will separate immediately.

To prevent jars and other glass vessels from cracking when boiling liquid is poured into them, stand a silver spoon in them before pouring in the liquid.

New glass tumblers, jugs, etc. will be less likely to crack if they are put into cold water and then brought to the boil before being used for the first time.

Gloves

Leather gloves can be kept soft after washing if a few drops of salad oil are mixed with the soapy water. Rinse lightly in warm water and dry flat in a towel. Hang the gloves after blowing into them to give them shape.

To clean kid gloves (of any colour), take some skimmed milk, white soap and a sponge. Dip the sponge lightly in the skimmed milk and then rub it on the soap. Put your hand in the glove to be cleaned and rub the glove all over with the sponge, repeating this procedure twice on the dirty part. The glove will clean perfectly.

Glue

To make a quick and safe glue for young children, mix flour and water to a thin paste.

Hangers

If you are short of hangers for trousers or skirts without loops, put two clothes pegs on an ordinary wire hanger.

Heat

To increase the heat in a room, aluminium foil taped on the walls behind the radiators will reflect the heat and make quite a difference to the temperature.

Hems

If you have no one to help you mark a skirt that you want to take up or down, stretch a string between two chairs at the height required and rub the string with a piece of chalk. Put on your dress or skirt and turn slowly and carefully, touching the string all the way round the skirt. The hem will be marked by the chalk at the perfect height.

Ironing

You will get a better and quicker result when ironing if you put a strip of aluminium foil the length of the ironing board underneath the padded cover. The foil will become hot and your clothes will be heated from both above and below.

If you have to stop ironing before you have ironed all the articles you have dampened, keep the remainder in a plastic bag until you are ready to press them. Don't leave them damp for too long.

Ironing symbols on garments

	Cool iron	For acrylics, triacetate, polyester, nylon and silk.
	Warm iron	For wool, wool and nylon mixtures, polyester and cotton mixtures.
	Hot iron	For cotton, linen, viscose.
	Do not iron	

Hooks

Self-adhesive wall hooks will not come unstuck if you coat the sticky side with clear nail varnish before you put the hooks up.

Horn

To clean horn, wash with soapy water and then wax with a natural-colour wax or a little almond oil. Leave for half an hour before polishing vigorously with a soft cloth.

Hot-water bottles

The safest way to fill a rubber hot-water bottle is to put it flat on the table, holding the neck upright. This will prevent hot water spurting up, which is caused by air in the bottle when it is filled in an upright position.

Hot-water bottles will last twice as long if a few drops of glycerine are added to the hot water when they are first filled. The glycerine will prevent the rubber from hardening so easily.

Irons

To remove starch sticking to the iron, or to remove the sticky patch left after scorching a fabric, sprinkle a piece of paper with fine kitchen salt and rub the iron backwards and forwards over it until the base becomes smooth again. You can also rub the iron with half a lemon dipped in fine kitchen salt.

Steam irons can get furred unless you use distilled water or water which has been boiled for half an hour and left to cool so that the chalk settles at the bottom.

To remove fur, half-fill the iron with vinegar. Warm the iron and press the steam button until all the vinegar has evaporated, then fill the iron with distilled or boiled water and steam it out again until the iron is dry. The iron will be clean inside and ready to be used again.

A few drops of your favourite toilet water mixed with the water inside your steam iron will perfume your linen delicately.

Ivory

To clean very dirty ivory, soak for a few hours in milk and then wash with warm soapy water. Hydrogen peroxide is also effective.

To remove marks from ivory, rub on furniture cream and then polish with a clean soft cloth.

To clean carved ivory, moisten a soft toothbrush in a little warm water and then dip it in denture-cleaning powder (obtainable from chemists). Rub the object gently. Rinse with warm water and dry carefully.

Discoloured ivory handles will regain their original whiteness if you rub them with half a lemon dipped in salt. Wash in warm water.

The white notes of a piano should be rubbed gently with methylated spirit. Avoid using water. Keep the keyboard uncovered as ivory gets yellow more quickly in the dark.

Ivory and bone

Cracked ivory or bone objects can be restored by submerging them in melted candlewax for a few minutes. Take them out, wipe off any surplus wax and leave to set. After this treatment the objects should be kept away from heat.

Jeans

To get rid of the white hem-line when lengthening old jeans, trousers, jackets or skirts, apply a mixture of ink and water in equal quantities. If it is too dark, apply water with the toothbrush until you get the right colour.

Jewellery

Jeweller's rouge is commonly used for cleaning silver or gold jewellery, but the following will do as well: apply toothpaste on an old toothbrush and rinse well afterwards, or soak in methylated spirit.

To clean very delicate gold or silver jewellery, leave it to soak overnight in 90 per cent alcohol and then dry in some bran.

Kettles

When a kettle is furred up, pour in a small quantity of vinegar (in the case of an electric kettle, the vinegar must cover the element). Warm the vinegar and shake it inside the kettle – if necessary repeat the operation – then rinse well.

A marble in a kettle will prevent furring.

Knives

To remove stains from steel knives, rub on a little scouring powder moistened with lemon juice.

Lace

To clean delicate old lace, spread it on a piece of white blotting paper. In a saucepan gently heat some potato flour until quite hot and then spread a thick layer of the hot flour over the lace, pressing it down with your fingers. Leave until cool and then remove with a soft brush. Repeat the operation if necessary.

Lacquer

To clean lacquer, never use a wet cloth as the dampness could make the lacquer peel. Apply a household spot remover with a dry cloth and then dry the object immediately.

Lamé fabric

Gold or silver lamé fabric can be kept shiny if it is regularly rubbed gently with a chamois skin. If the fabric is dull-looking, rub with a very warm piece of crustless bread. Repeat the operation until the lamé shines again, or rub the fabric with warm bran and then finish shining with the chamois skin.

Lead

When storing lead figures, etc., keep them in a polythene bag as lead can be attacked by acidic organic vapours from wood if kept in a wooden cupboard.

To clean lead figures, boil them in two or three changes of water for 5 minutes at a time and then put them in a container with 8 parts of water to 1 part vinegar. Soak for a short time, then rinse in water containing a small quantity of washing soda. Rinse again in plain water and dry carefully.

Leather

See *Gloves* on page 78.

Letters

Letters or packets cannot be steamed open if sealed with the white of an egg.

Lids

When a lid sticks and refuses to come off, a rubber band put tightly around it will provide a good grip for the hand and allow the lid to be removed successfully. If all else fails, dip the top of the jar in boiling water for a few minutes and the lid should be loosened.

Light bulbs

Long-life bulbs last for about 2000 hours. They cost more and shed less light than other bulbs.

Normal bulbs have a life expectancy of 1000 hours.

Pearl bulbs cast softer shadows, and throw no shadow on the ceiling.

Clear bulbs do cast shadows.

Pink pearl bulbs give a warm glow without any appreciable loss of light.

A few drops of your favourite perfume rubbed on to a light bulb will fill the room with a delicate scent when the light is on.

Linen

Fine linen that is not in constant use should be wrapped in blue tissue paper. This preserves the colour and stops the linen becoming yellow.

To distinguish linen from cotton, wet a fingertip and apply it to the material. If it is cotton the moisture will take some time to show on the other side; if it is linen, this will show immediately.

Marble

To clean marble, apply hydrogen peroxide to the stain. Leave for 10 minutes and then rinse off.

Another method is to use a cut lemon (if the marble is stained, dip the lemon in salt first). Restore the gloss with 1½ pints (1 litre) of hot water mixed with 3 tablespoons of vinegar.

Matches

If you have damp matches that will not light, dip them in nail varnish and strike. You do not have to wait for the varnish to dry.

Mats

A mat placed inside the house next to each outer door will help to keep the house clean.

To keep the edges of a mat or carpet from curling up, paste some very thick starch along the edge and then iron over some brown paper with a fairly hot iron.

Mirrors

For a way to avoid steamed-up mirrors, see *Windows* on page 101.

Mosquitoes

Candles placed on the table during outdoor meals will discourage mosquitoes.

Moths

Epsom salts are a good deterrent to moths, so sprinkle the crystals amongst clothing, furs, etc. in wardrobes and drawers.

Soap placed in wardrobes and drawers is also an effective deterrent.

Nappies

If nappies are still in good condition when the baby has grown up, dye them different colours and use them as small towels.

Net curtains

Buy one and a half times or twice the length of the track if you want full curtains.

Newspaper

To light a fire, newspaper is an effective substitute for wood if it is rolled into a long thin tube and knotted in the middle.

Oilcloth

To make oilcloth as new again, lightly beat the white of an egg and rub it over the oilcloth with a soft cloth. Leave it to dry and then polish with a dry cloth.

To remove marks left by hot plates, rub the marks with a cloth dipped in camphor oil.

Oil lamp

To make an oil lamp in an emergency, fill a drinking glass two-thirds full with water and pour on some cooking oil to form a layer on top. Cut a thick disc from a cork and make a hole in the centre of it, large enough to hold a wick made from 10 to 12 strands of cotton thread knotted together. The wick should stick out 1 inch (2 cm) on both sides of the disc. Float the disc on the oil, light the wick and you will have a lamp glowing in your hand.

Ormolu (French gilt)

To clean ormolu, never use metal polish. Wash with vinegar and water, rinse and dry.

To remove tarnish, brush gently with soapy water containing a few drops of ammonia and then rinse and dry.

Paint

To remove paint from your hands, rub them with some salad oil. This method will be gentle on your skin, too.

Paint brushes

To soften brushes which have hardened, immerse them in hot vinegar.

Painting

When decorating, stretch a thin piece of wire across the top of your tin of paint so that you can wipe your brush against it after dipping into the paint.

Paintings

Oil paintings which are not of great value can be cleaned at home by rubbing gently with a piece of cottonwool dampened with white spirit. Treat one small area at a time.

Pans

To remove scaling from a pan, rub with steel wool dipped first in vinegar and then in salt.

To remove burnt food, cover with baking soda, moisten with hot water and leave to stand. Or add a larger amount of water and boil the mixture in the pan.

To clean pans made of tin, iron or steel (but not aluminium), fill two-thirds full with a solution of washing soda (1 tablespoon to 1 pint or ½ litre of water). Bring to the boil and boil slowly for 10 minutes. Rinse well.

To remove rust, dip a piece of raw potato in a mild abrasive and rub the stain with it. Do not use scouring powder as it removes the tin coating from iron or steel pans.

Paper hanging

Paste the wall instead of the wallpaper – you will find the paper much easier to hang.

Papier mâché

To make papier mâché, tear some cardboard egg cartons into small pieces. Put these into a container and cover with cold water. Leave them to get soft and then, with your fingers, work to a smooth mixture. Squeeze out the excess water and add some adhesive (e.g. wallpaper paste) to form about ⅛ of the mixture. Mix well and then keep the papier mâché in tied plastic bags. It can be kept for up to 2 days before use.

Parcels

When tying up a parcel, first dip the string in warm water and then tie and knot as usual. As the string dries, it will shrink and make the knot very tight.

Patent leather

To clean patent-leather shoes and handbags, rub gently with cottonwool dipped in almond oil and then shine with a soft dry cloth.

To maintain patent leather, rub vaseline into it regularly.

Pearls

Real or cultured pearls can be distinguished by biting them. If they feel gritty to the teeth, they are genuine.

Real or cultured pearls should be worn as often as possible because contact with the skin gives them a brilliance and maintains their natural colour.

To clean a pearl necklace, leave it submerged overnight in powdered magnesia and gently brush away the powder in the morning.

Pewter

Pewter is easily dented because it is a soft metal (an alloy of tin and lead), so when cleaning it never use a metal-cleaning powder or liquid. Gently wash it in warm, soapy water and then dry and polish with a soft chamois or cloth.

To remove bad stains, rub with the finest steel wool dipped in olive oil. The oil will prevent steel wool making scratches on the pewter.

Never store pewter in an oak cupboard, as oak gives off fumes which corrode the pewter.

Photographs

To clean photographs, use cottonwool dipped in methylated spirit so as not to damage the surface.

Pillows

Real down is the best filling for a pillow as it has the right amount of resistance, moulding comfortably to the head and springing back into shape when the head is removed. It is expensive, but will last for a very long time.

A filling of goose feathers and down makes the pillow firmer, but is still a very satisfactory mixture and much cheaper than real down.

Goose feathers make the best feather filling as they are not as heavy as hen feathers.

When buying a pillow with a loose filling, shake it from one end. If all the filling drops down to the other end, it means that the pillow will flatten quickly when in use.

Pingpong balls

If pingpong balls are dented but not cracked, they can be restored by dropping them into boiling water to which a pinch of salt has been added. Stir the balls for a few minutes and the dents will disappear.

Plastic bottles

For easy disposal, pour a small quantity of boiling water into the bottle. The plastic will become soft and the bottle will collapse – you can then just crush it in your hands.

Pressing trousers

Creases in trousers can be sharpened by rubbing the wrong side of the crease with a dry piece of soap.

Quilts

The best quilts are those filled with the largest amount of good down as this is light, warm and very resilient. They are expensive, but well worth buying as they will last for a lifetime.

Down quilts contain up to 15 per cent of their weight of small feathers.

Down and feather quilts must contain at least 51 per cent of down.

Feather and down quilts consist mainly of feathers and should contain at least 15 per cent of down.

Rocking chairs

Some rocking chairs have a tendency to move all over the floor when used. A good strong velvet ribbon (nylon velvet will do) glued to the rockers will prevent this.

Rubber gloves

If you have long nails, put a piece of cottonwool in each fingertip of rubber gloves to prevent your nails piercing the rubber.

The right hand usually wears out first, so keep the left hand for the next pair: when the right hand glove goes again, turn the spare left-hand glove inside out and you will have a right-hand glove.

Old rubber gloves can be made into rubber bands of different sizes

by cutting across the double thickness over and over again, including the fingers.

Rubber protectors

Use rubber protectors on top of your draining board and on the end of the tap to save you from cracked and chipped crockery, china and glasses.

Rust

To clean rust off steel or iron, first soften the rust by dipping the object in paraffin for 24 hours. Then take it out of the paraffin, wipe it lightly and rub the metal with steel wool until clean. If it is not possible to dip the object, wrap the rusty part with a cloth soaked in paraffin and leave it for 24 hours. Then rub the metal with steel wool. Protect non-metal parts with plastic adhesive tape.

To remove rust marks from a steel draining board, rub with lighter fluid.

Saucepans

When buying a new saucepan, at the same time buy an enamel dish

which fits on top. When you use the saucepan you can place the dish on top of it and steam left-over food to re-heat it without using extra fuel.

Screws

To make it easier to insert a screw into hard wood, put wax polish or candlewax on the end of the screw.

To remove a rusty screw, if oil has failed, apply a little vinegar and leave it for a few minutes to penetrate before using a screwdriver.

Serving trolley

Invest in a serving trolley: it will be very useful, not only for serving meals but also for carrying all sorts of things throughout the house.

Sewing

When sewing buttons on to thick material, a matchstick placed underneath or across the top of the button will ensure the correct shank. It is also helpful if you use elastic thread instead of cotton.

When sewing plastic with a sewing machine, put a piece of

greaseproof paper between the needle and the plastic. This will stop the plastic puckering or being cut. Tear away the greaseproof paper when you have finished sewing.

Sheepskin linings

To clean white sheepskin lining, rub with a sponge dampened in liquid detergent.

Sheets

To make fitted sheets, tie a knot in each corner of a plain sheet and tuck the knot well under the mattress.

With a laundry marker, write an S or a D in one corner of all your sheets so that you can see at a glance which are single and which are double.

Shoes

Shoe trees are very important, so insert them whenever you take off your shoes. Paper stuffed into the shoe will do as second best.

To prevent slipping, scratch the sole of new leather-soled shoes with a knife or pair of scissors.

If a leather shoe is tight, put it on, dip a cloth in hot water and lay it across the shoe. Repeat this operation several times: the moist heat will make the leather shape itself to the foot.

Brown shoes can be darkened and cleaned by rubbing them with the inside of a banana skin or a cut potato. Leave to dry and then polish with a soft cloth.

Remove stains from brown shoes with a few drops of lemon juice or vinegar mixed with a few drops of water.

Marks on light suede shoes can be removed by rubbing talcum powder into the stains and leaving overnight.

Rain spots on suede shoes can be removed by rubbing the shoes with fine glasspaper when they are dry.

The rope heels of canvas shoes can be cleaned by brushing with a carpet shampoo. Rinse and leave to dry.

Sea-water stains on shoes can be removed by dissolving a small piece of washing soda in a few tablespoons of hot milk. While the mixture is warm, apply it to the stains with a cloth, rubbing well. When dry, clean the shoes with your usual polish.

Shoe polish that is caked, hard or lumpy can be softened with a few drops of paraffin, turpentine or olive oil.

Silk

To renovate black silk, slice some raw potatoes and pour boiling water over them. When cold, sponge the right side of the silk with this liquid and iron on the wrong side.

To iron out all the creases and press silk smoothly, first sprinkle it with water and roll up tightly in a towel. Leave for at least an hour. Do not use too hot an iron as it will make the colour run.

Silver

When storing silver or silver plate, wrap it in a plastic bag – it will keep clean much longer.

A piece of camphor in the drawer or cupboard where silver is stored will keep it bright.

Do not let rubber touch your silver, as it will leave ugly black marks.

Egg tarnish on silver is quickly removed by rubbing it with table salt.

To remove a salt stain, rub it with damp salt – this works like magic.

Acid stains are difficult to remove, but will disappear if rubbed with salt and a few drops of lemon juice.

If your silver salt cellars have no linings, the salt should be removed after use. If they are lined, make sure that no salt is lodged between the silver and the linings. Remove the spoon from the salt cellar after every meal.

Table silver should be washed in soapy water with 1 tablespoon of ammonia (or vinegar). Rinse in hot water and dry. This method will keep the silver in good condition and it will only need occasional treatment with a silver cleaner.

To clean silver in a hurry, apply some methylated spirit with a rag. Leave the silver to dry for a few minutes and then polish with a soft cloth.

Table cutlery and table silver should always be washed after cleaning to avoid the cleaning product contaminating the food.

Home dip for silver: an easy and unmessy way to get your silver shining. Crumple a piece of aluminium foil in a large container with some washing soda and pour boiling water over it. (Some fumes may be given off but this is a normal electrochemical reaction so do not worry.) Immerse the silver and leave until the tarnish has been removed, then rinse and dry. The solution does not need to be strong – 2 tablespoons of washing soda to 1 gallon (4 litres) of water.

To give lustre to new silver, dip it in very hot water to heat the metal, then quickly dip it in bleach, dry it and clean with silver polish to bring out the reliefs.

Silver gilt

Silver gilt is silver coated with gold. It should be cleaned with soapy water. Do not use a silver polish, as this would remove the gold.

Silver plate

Silver plate is either nickel or Britannia metal coated with silver. The best has a nickel base, with the stamp E.P.N.S. (electroplated nickel silver). The stamp E.P.B.M. means electroplated Britannia metal. Britannia metal is a mixture of tin, copper, zinc and antimony.

Sheffield plate is very valuable because of its rarity. It has a copper base with a silver coating.

Soap

To harden and prolong its life, do not use your soap straight after buying it. If you store it in a cupboard in its original packaging for a while, it will harden and last longer when used.

To make a scented soap, save all the small scraps, put them in a jar and stand the jar in boiling water until the scraps melt. Pour in a few drops of your favourite perfume, mix well, and when it starts to cool remove from the jar and knead into the desired shape.

Socks

Knee-high stretch-nylon socks make ideal shoe bags for travelling.

Sponges

To clean a sponge, place it overnight in a bowl of water to which lemon juice or vinegar has been added (½ pint or 300 ml of water to 5 tablespoons of lemon juice or vinegar). Remove the sponge and rinse well; it will be very clean and as good as new.

To both clean and soften a sponge, soak it in salted water overnight, or soak it for a few hours in buttermilk and then rinse in clean water.

Stainless steel

To clean stainless steel, rub it with a soft cloth dampened in vinegar. Dry with a soft cloth.

Steel

To polish steel, mix the juice of an onion with three times the quantity of vinegar. Keep this in a jar. Dab the steel with the mixture, leave for 20 minutes and then shine with a soft cloth.

Steel wool

To stop steel wool rusting after use, store in a solution of 1 cup of water and a tablespoon of baking soda.

Stockings

Save laddered stockings or tights, cut them into shreds and use to stuff cushions and toys.

Stoppers

To loosen glass stoppers, pour on a little vinegar and then turn the stopper sharply.

To loosen the stopper of a perfume bottle, immerse the bottle in a jar of vinegar, leave for a short while and then take it out and stand it in warm water. The stopper will soon loosen.

Straw hats

Methylated spirit is excellent for restoring colour and shape to straw hats. After dusting the straw, apply methylated spirit with a pad of cottonwool – it will also give the required stiffness.

Suede

Shine on suede can be removed by rubbing the shiny area with fine emery paper.

Suits

A solution of vinegar and water in equal quantities is excellent for removing the shine.

Tablecloths

If a tablecloth is stained during a meal, cover it with a layer of salt. This will remove most of the stain and make it easier to launder.

Teapots

When a teapot or teacup is badly stained, rub it with salt.

When a silver teapot is not in use, keep a lump of sugar inside to keep it dry and prevent mustiness.

Thermos flasks

Thermos flasks become stained after long use. To clean them, put in half an eggshell and 2 tablespoons of vinegar. Stand for a few minutes and then shake vigorously, add a glass of warm water and shake well again. The flask should then be quite clean.

To get rid of the smell of coffee and coffee stains, pour in a cup of boiling water and 1 tablespoon of raw rice, shake for a few minutes and rinse.

Tiles

Before laying plastic, cork or linoleum tiles, warm them in a cool oven (275°F, 135°C, Gas Mark 1). Tiles are brittle when cold, and easily break or split when being cut to fit.

Toothbrushes

Old toothbrushes are very useful for cleaning around taps.

Torn fabric

Place the torn part flat on a table, spread the wrong side with an egg white, place a piece of the same fabric or a piece of fine linen on top and press with a hot iron. The tear will be almost invisible and the repair will last for quite a time.

Tortoiseshell

To clean tortoiseshell, moisten a little jeweller's rouge with a few drops of salad oil, rub it gently over the object with cottonwool, then shine with a soft cloth.

Trousers

To remove shine marks from *dark* trousers, pour hot water over used coffee grounds, dip a cloth in the mixture and rub trousers with it.

Underwear

If your nylon underwear has gone grey, dye it flesh-colour by dipping it in a strong, strained brew of tea. Simmer, stirring, until the underwear is the desired colour.

Velvet

To restore the flattened pile of velvet, cover a hot iron with a wet cloth and hold the velvet firmly over it. Or hold the velvet, stretched tight, over boiling water.

Wallpaper

To remove blisters from wallpaper, fill a syringe with paste and inject into the blister. Allow a few minutes for the paper to absorb the paste, and then gently flatten the blister with your fingers. Go over it with a roller to give a good finish.

To strip wallpaper, dissolve some alum in a bucket of warm water, as much as the water will take. Soak the wall thoroughly with it – it can be applied with a roller or a good-sized paintbrush. When it is dry, the paper will peel off effortlessly.

Wallpaper makes a very pretty gift wrap, especially at Christmas time when you need large quantities. It works out much less expensive than wrapping paper.

See also *Paper hanging* on page 88.

Washing and dry-cleaning symbols on garments
Washing

Do not wash   Hand-wash only   Do not use chlorine bleach   Chlorine bleach can be used

Temperatures given on the international symbols are in degrees centigrade.

	Machine	Hand	
1 95	Very hot	Hand-hot 50°C/120°F	White linen and cotton without special finishes.
2 60	Hot	Hand-hot 50°C/120°F	Colourfast linen and cotton without special finishes.
3 60	Hot	Hand-hot 50°C/120°F	White nylon, white polyester-cotton mixtures.
4 50	Hand-hot	Hand-hot 50°C/120°F	Coloured nylon; polyester; acrylic-cotton mixtures; cotton rayon with special finishes; coloured polyester-cotton mixtures.
5 40	Warm	Warm 40°C/100°F	Non-colourfast linen, cotton or rayon.
6 40	Warm	Warm 40°C/100°F	Acrylics; acetates; blends of these fabrics with wool; mixtures of wool and polyester.
7 40	Warm	Warm 40°C/100°F	Wool; silk; wool mixtures with cotton or rayon.
8 30	Cool	Cool 30°C/85°F	Silk; acetate fabrics with colours not fast at higher temperatures.
9 95	Very hot	Hand-hot 50°C/120°F	Cotton can be boiled but requires dripdrying.

Dry-cleaning

These symbols tell your cleaner which dry-cleaning agents are suitable.

   Do not dry-clean.

Washing machines

One teacup of white vinegar added to the last rinse in your washing machine will make sure your clothes are well rinsed. The vinegar also acts as a softener.

If you put too much washing powder in your washing machine and it overflows, sprinkle with salt. The suds will quickly subside.

Water

To test if water is safe to drink, the simplest way is to fill a glass of water, put a lump of sugar into it and leave the glass in a warm room either overnight or for 24 hours. If the water is clear at the end of the time, then it is quite pure, but if it is cloudy or milky then it is unfit to drink.

Make sure that everyone in the family knows where the mains water tap is and how to turn it off in case of emergency.

Water marks

To remove dry chalk marks from vases, jugs, bottles and glass use malt vinegar. Leave for a few hours, or more if the marks are bad, then rub off with a fine wire scouring pad.

Wicks

To prevent wicks from smoking, soak in vinegar before use.

Windows

Do not clean windows when the sun is shining on them as they will look streaky when they dry.

Use a solution of equal parts of water and methylated spirit in a bottle. Shake well, damp a newspaper with the solution and rub on windows or mirrors. Polish with a soft cloth.

When cleaning both the inside and outside of a window, use horizontal strokes on one side and vertical strokes on the other. In this way you will know on which side any smudges are.

To prevent frosty or steamy windows and mirrors, clean in the usual way and then apply a small quantity of glycerine with a soft, clean cloth, rubbing lightly but well. The glass will stay clean for weeks.

Paint on windows can be removed with hot vinegar or a razor blade.

To make a sash window run smoothly, rub the sash cord thoroughly with soft soap.

When painting window frames, the best way to avoid getting paint on the glass is to use a piece of cardboard laid flat on the glass and held close to the frame.

Wooden floors

Wooden floors will turn yellow after a while if very hot water, strong soaps and soda are used to clean them. Plain wood is absorbent, so never use excessive amounts of water when washing it as the grain will open too much.

Wooden tables

Unvarnished wooden tables should be rubbed frequently with salad oil. Rub any stains with a very fine steel wool and rinse well afterwards.

Varnished tables should also be rubbed with salad oil from time to time to avoid the wood becoming dry and brittle-looking.

Woollens

When your woollen garments have been washed in water that is too hot and they become hard and 'felted', wash them in warm water to which glycerine has been added (1½ tablespoons to 1¾ pints or about 1 litre). Then rinse very thoroughly in warm water.

Wrought iron

To keep wrought iron in good condition, brush it with natural wax and then shine.

Zip fasteners

If a zip is not running properly, a little soft soap or candlewax rubbed on it will have an immediate effect.

Stains

Stains on fabric

Some fabrics and colours can be damaged by certain solvents or spirits, so always test a small corner of the fabric first (leave for 20 minutes).

Always rinse the fabric after removing a stain, or rub it with a piece of cottonwool dampened in cold water, to remove all traces of spirit or solvent.

Do not use water-based solutions on non-washable fabrics.

When removing stains from fabrics, start from the edge of the stain and work towards the centre. This will prevent the stain spreading.

A simple rule for unknown stains on fabric: first rub the stain with cold water. If the stain persists, rub on a mixture of lemon juice and salt. If this has no effect, rub on bicarbonate of soda; if this also fails, dab the area with methylated spirit.

Ballpoint or felt-tip ink

These stains will disappear if rubbed with methylated or surgical spirit.

Blood

Washable fabric: bloodstains should always be cleaned with cold water, as hot water makes the marks permanent. Soak in cool water for a while and then wash in warm soapy water. If the stain still persists, soak the material in warm water with a little bleach.

Non-washable fabric: put a clean cloth underneath the stain and sponge lightly with hydrogen peroxide or ammonia.

Silk, satin or crêpe de Chine: make a thick paste of starch and water, cover the stain with it and leave to dry completely. Brush the starch off with a soft brush. The stain will have disappeared and no harm will have been done to the fabric.

Candle grease

First remove as much as possible with a blunt instrument, then place blotting paper over the stain and press it with a hot iron, moving the paper frequently until no more grease appears on it.

Chewing gum

Scrape off as much as possible with a knife, then rub it with an ice-cube and scrape with the knife again. Then use methylated spirit or dry-cleaning fluid to finish.

Chocolate, cocoa, coffee

Washable fabric: wash in lukewarm soapy water. If the stain persists, soak the fabric for a few minutes in a mild bleach or rub with glycerine. Leave it for 1 hour and then wash in soapy water again.

Non-washable fabric: first sponge with lukewarm water. If the stain persists, rub with a small sponge or pad of cottonwool which has been first dampened with water then squeezed and dipped in methylated spirit or ammonia.

Deodorant

Use a solution of white vinegar rubbed on with a cloth or sponge. If the stain is persistent, try methylated spirit.

Fruit

Washable fabric: place the stained fabric over a container and pour boiling water through the stain. Soap must not be used. If the stain is old, soften it by rubbing with glycerine first, let it stand for 2 to 3 hours and then treat with boiling water.

Non-washable fabric: first dab the stain with white vinegar, then sponge lightly with cold water. Or dab the stain with cold water and then sprinkle with bicarbonate of soda. Leave it on for about 15 minutes, then brush it off and leave it to dry.

Glue

Dab with cottonwool dampened in a mixture of 2 spoons of warm water to 5 spoons of vinegar.

Grass

Washable fabric: soak in warm soapy water. If the stain persists, use a mild bleach.

Non-washable fabric: sponge with a solution of methylated spirit (or surgical spirit) and water in equal proportions.

Grease

To remove fresh stains, spread a layer of talcum powder over them and press it on gently with your fingers. When the talcum becomes caked, brush it off. Repeat this until most of the stain has been removed and then apply another layer and leave it overnight.

Washable fabric: treat first with dry-cleaning fluid or methylated spirit. Then wash in warm soapy water.

Non-washable fabric: put some blotting paper on the ironing board, spread the stained fabric over the paper and place another piece of blotting paper on top of the stain. Press lightly with a warm iron. Change the blotting paper when soiled. When most of the stain has been absorbed, sponge with dry-cleaning fluid or ammonia.

Silk: make a lump of magnesia (powder of magnesia mixed with water) and rub it on the spots. Let it dry and then brush off.

Ink

Washable fabric: dip the stained part in cold water and then lay the fabric over a bowl. Cover the stain with a good layer of salt and squeeze the juice of a lemon over it. Leave for at least 2 hours and then wash in the usual way.

Non-washable fabric: dab the stain with a solution of peroxide and water in equal proportions, or with cloudy ammonia (1 tablespoon to ½ pint or 300ml of water).

Linen: rub with a ripe tomato and the stain will soon disappear. Then wash the linen in lukewarm water. Another method is to spread freshly made mustard over the stain, leaving it for half an hour before rinsing off.

Iron burns

Place the burned part over a small container of boiling water. Make a paste with 2 teaspoons of fine salt and 2 teaspoons of lemon juice. Rub the stain gently with the mixture, then rinse with warm water.

Lipstick

Washable fabric: work vaseline into the stain, then wash in the usual way. If the stain persists, soak the fabric in a mild bleach for a few minutes.

Non-washable fabric: rub gently with dry-cleaning fluid.

Milk

Washable fabric: soak for a while in lukewarm water and then wash in the usual way.

Non-washable fabric: sponge the stain with dry-cleaning fluid and then sponge with lukewarm water.

Mud

Washable fabric: wait until the mud is dry, then brush off as much as you can and wash in soapy water.

Non-washable fabric: sponge the stain with methylated spirit (or surgical spirit) and water in equal proportions.

Nail varnish

Place pad underneath the stain and rub gently with cottonwool dampened with acetone. Do not use acetone on acetate fabric; the chemically pure amyl acetate should be used (obtainable from chemists).

Paint

Washable fabric: if the stain is fresh, soften with some salad oil, turpentine or white spirit and then wash in warm soapy water.

Non-washable fabric: soften the stain with turpentine or white spirit and then apply dry-cleaning fluid.

Fresh emulsion paint can be washed off with cold water. Cellulose paint can be removed with acetone. To remove oil or enamel paints turpentine should be used: place a pad of cottonwool underneath the stain to absorb the paint and use another cottonwool pad to clean. Change both pads frequently.

Perfume

Washable fabric: gently rub the stain with a pad of cottonwool dampened in white spirit. Then wash in warm soapy water.

Non-washable fabric: gently rub the stain with a pad of cottonwool dampened in white spirit. If the stain persists, rub it gently with hydrogen peroxide and sponge with cold water. For acetate fabrics use 1 part of white spirit to 2 parts water.

Perspiration

Washable fabric: do not wash the garment until the stains have been treated. Soak the affected part in cold water for half an hour, then rub half a juicy lemon on it and let it soak in for a minute or two. Rinse and wash as usual. Sometimes the colour can be restored by holding the fabric, first dampened in water, over the fumes of an open bottle of cloudy ammonia.

Non-washable fabric: sponge the stain gently with a solution of cloudy ammonia and water in equal quantities.

Rust

Washable fabric: rub the stain with half a lemon dipped in salt and then wash in the usual way.

Non-washable fabric: rub the stain with half a lemon dipped in salt and then sponge with cold water.

Scorch marks

Quickly dampen a piece of cottonwool in peroxide and rub the scorch gently.

Another method is to moisten a piece of sugar with water, rub the scorch slightly and sponge with cold water.

Tea

Washable fabric: old stains can be removed by applying lemon juice before washing the fabric in warm soapy water.

Non-washable fabric: put some lemon juice on the stain, leave it for a while and then sponge with cold water. Or sponge the stain lightly with a solution of peroxide and water in equal quantities.

Water

Rain spots on fabrics such as velvet, felt and taffeta can be removed by holding the fabric in the steam from a boiling kettle (not too near the spout).

Satin: rub gently with tissue paper in a circular motion.

Wine

Washable fabric: loosen the stain with glycerine and then wash in warm soapy water.

Non-washable fabric: sponge with a solution of peroxide and water in equal quantities.

Red-wine stains will disappear if white wine is applied to them. Afterwards, sponge with warm water.

Stains on leather

If leather is stained, rub it gently with a soft rag dipped in white spirit.

Ink

To remove ink stains from leather, use lemon juice. It will take a little of the colour away, so use shoe polish to bring the colour back.

To clean ballpoint stains on leather or fabric use 90 per cent alcohol or the 'Efflax' pen used by schoolchildren.

Stains on carpets

Ink

Rub plenty of warm milk into the stain, then sponge with warm water.

First mop with blotting paper, then rub with a cloth or sponge wrung out in a mixture of water and vinegar in equal quantities.

Old stains can be removed if sprinkled with salt and rubbed with half a lemon. Then sponge with vinegar.

Another method is to rub the stain with methylated spirit or surgical spirit.

Red ink is more difficult to remove, but try rubbing with a thick paste of borax and water. If the stain persists, rub lightly with methylated spirit or surgical spirit.

Soot

Never wet a soot stain. Cover the stain with salt and brush it off with a stiff brush. Repeat the process until the stain has disappeared.

Wine

Red wine will disappear if you put white wine on it.

Use soda water to remove red or white wine, then sponge with cold water.

Stains on linoleum

Use ether or white spirit. Do not use coarse detergent.

Stains on wood

Blood

Rub with peroxide.

Cigarette burns

First sandpaper gently with the finest abrasive paper, rubbing away the black burned wood. Then, with a cottonwool bud dipped in household bleach, dab the burn in order to bleach it. Leave to dry, then polish with a shoe polish the colour of the wood.

Grease

Sprinkle with coarse salt as soon as the stain appears to prevent the grease sinking into the wood.

Heat marks

Mahogany: rub the mark well with a piece of cloth dipped in linseed oil, then polish with a soft cloth.

Polished tables: make a paste with linseed oil and salt and coat the mark thickly. Leave it for a good hour, remove and then polish in the usual way. Another method is to mix some cigarette (or, better still, cigar) ashes with a few drops of salad oil to make a thick paste. Rub over the mark gently until it disappears, then wax and polish with a soft cloth.

Ink

Rub the stain with a cloth dampened in vinegar and methylated spirit in equal quantities.

Water

If the mark is only slight, rub it with a metal polish then use wax polish to shine the surface again.

If water has penetrated the wood, mix equal parts of linseed oil and turpentine and rub into the mark with a soft cloth.

Stains on wallpaper

Finger marks and other light stains can be removed by rubbing with a ball of bread.

Grease

Spray some starch over the stain, leave to dry and then brush gently with a clean soft brush. Or rub the stain with a warm iron over blotting paper.

Plants

The Garden

Ants

To prevent ants climbing, rub a good thick coating of chalk around the plant or object to be protected (walls, pipes, wooden posts, etc.) – ants cannot walk on chalk. Renew every few weeks.

Broccoli

Thyme or mint planted near broccoli will discourage cabbage moths.

Cabbage

To stop the head of a cabbage or cauliflower cracking open, make an

incision in the stalk on one side, beneath the head, and insert a small piece of wood into the cut.

Thyme or mint planted near cabbages will discourage cabbage moths.

Radishes planted near cabbages discourage maggots.

Carrots

To discourage the carrot fly, plant onions next to carrots. Both carrot fly *and* onion fly will avoid the plot.

Coffee grounds

Don't throw away your coffee grounds: put them on the soil in your garden or in your plant pots, because they serve the same purpose as tea-leaves.

Flowers

The best time to pick flowers from the garden is in the early morning or early evening. Do not pick them during the warmest part of the day, because this is when the plant is at its lowest sweating point and the flowers would not last very long.

Do not pick flowers in full bloom as the petals will fall very quickly. Choose half-opened blooms, and always leave your freshly picked or bought flowers standing in a deep container full of water in a cool place for at least 3 hours, more if possible, standing up to their necks in water.

When buying flowers, avoid any that have been standing in the sun, or any from which the pollen is dropping.

Arranging flowers

To arrange cut flowers in a bowl, fill the bowl with sand to within an inch of the top and soak with water. The flowers will stay fresh and upright twice as long.

Flower holder: cut a slice from the base of a potato to make it sit squarely and then make holes to take the stems. The moisture from the potato will keep foliage fresh for many days without water in a shallow arrangement.

To keep the water pure in a vase, put a piece of charcoal at the bottom.

To keep flowers fresh, add a pinch of nitrate of soda every time the water is changed.

To make flowers last longer, put their stems into lukewarm water to which a spoon of salt has been added.

To revive limp flowers, cut ½ inch from the stems and plunge the freshly trimmed ends into boiling water at once. The flowers will resume their beauty in a surprisingly short time.

Cyclamen, tulips and other similar flowers are very decorative, but tend to droop. A little starch in the water will keep them upright for several days.

Flowers like daffodils and narcissi exude a sticky substance when cut, which makes drinking difficult for them. Before arranging them, hold the ends of the stems under warm running water to remove this juice.

Flowers with milky stems (e.g. dahlias, poinsettias and poppies) cannot absorb water until the milky juice has coagulated. To prevent bleeding, singe the end of the stem with a match just after cutting, or dip 2 inches (4 cm) of the stem in boiling water for 30 seconds.

Carnations: carnation stems should be broken between the joints to allow the flowers to drink more freely.

Hydrangeas: the flower head of a hydrangea absorbs water, so when arranging hydrangeas in a pot or vase spray the flower head or first soak it in cool water for a few seconds.

Lilac: the bark should be peeled off the stem below water-level or it will poison the water; the bottom inch (2 cm) of the stem should be hammered or split to allow the lilac to drink more freely and so last longer.

Lupins: these have hollow stems which, after being cut, should be filled with water and then blocked with a piece of cottonwool. Afterwards, put them in deep water for a few hours.

Mimosa: this needs to be sprayed two or three times a day to keep its fluffy look.

Roses: the stalks should be well bruised to make them last longer, or split with a knife about 1 inch (2 cm) up the stem.

Tulips: to allow cut tulips to drink freely and so live longer in a vase, pierce the stalk right through with a needle at ½ inch (1 cm) intervals from the head to the stem before putting the flowers in water.

Tulips have juicy stems and do not last as long as they should if mixed with other flowers in a vase.

A little table salt in the water will stop tulips opening fully in a vase and so make them last longer.

Wallflowers: being bushy, wallflowers are excellent for arrangements, but if they are to last their stems should be cut short.

To intensify the colours in a flower arrangement, include a touch of white (this applies to flowers in a garden, too).

Drying flowers

To dry flowers, cut them when in full bloom and dip the ends of the stalks in candlewax. Dry them, hanging upside down, in a gentle heat.

See also *Roses* on page 122.

Foliage

To preserve foliage, cut sprays and take them home before they wilt. Peel off a few inches of bark at the bottom and make a slit in the stems. Put the sprays into a deep container with salt and water (a handful of salt to a jar of water). Leave overnight, and then arrange the sprays in a vase the next day. The vase should contain a solution of equal parts of glycerine and water (cheap, crude glycerine will do) to fill the vase one-third full. This method will preserve the foliage for many months.

Frozen plants

To revive greenhouse plants which have become frozen, make it as dark as possible in the greenhouse and thaw the plants with cold water. If watered in the light, the plants would die.

Garlic

To grow one big, round clove of garlic instead of several small ones, plant the cloves in the second week of March. Garlic planted between October and February will produce a head of several smaller cloves.

Garlic planted near beans, lettuces, tomatoes, roses, etc. will discourage greenfly.

Grass

To stop grass growing between the stone slabs of a footpath in the garden, sprinkle salt in the interstices.

Greenfly

See *Pests and diseases* on page 120.

Herbs

Herbs can be grown together, except for fennel and dill. Mint develops its roots so quickly that there is no room left for other herbs, unless you restrain it by planting it in a large tin (e.g. a paint tin). Cut the top and bottom off the tin, and sink it into the soil.

To make herb plants thick and bushy, and to stop them growing too tall, pinch out the centre stem to encourage the side shoots to develop.

See also *Window boxes* on page 129.

Insecticide

A cheap insecticide can be made at home by mixing equal quantities of milk, paraffin and water. It is impossible to mix paraffin and water, but if you mix the milk and paraffin first the water will then blend easily into the solution.

Ladybirds

An adult ladybird eats about 100 greenflies a day, so leave ladybirds on your roses or fruit trees and do not use insecticide on them.

Leeks

To discourage maggots, from time to time place some egg shells on small sticks between the leeks – butterflies will lay their eggs on or inside the shells instead of the leeks.

Grow tomatoes between leeks as butterflies are repelled by their smell.

Mint

Mint planted with cabbage and broccoli will discourage cabbage moths.

Moss

Moss often turns a dirty light-green or yellowish colour when dried. To preserve its fresh green colour, dip the moss in a strong solution of washing blue for 1 minute. Remove it from the solution, squeeze it gently in your hands and leave to dry on newspaper. When completely dry, store in a brown-paper bag until needed.

Onions

To avoid onion fly, plant onions next to carrots (or better still *with* the carrots). Both types of fly will avoid the plot.

Pests and diseases

Greenfly

Greenfly accumulates on the underneath of the leaves and young shoots, making them look distorted and sticky. To get rid of greenfly, spray the whole plant (particularly the undersides of the leaves) twice a week with a weak soap-flake solution.

To discourage greenfly, plant garlic amongst the plants that attract it.

Mealy bugs

Mealy bugs attack both the undersides of leaves and the joints in the stem; they look like dots of cottonwool. Rub them off the plant with a cottonwool bud dipped in methylated spirit or white spirit.

Red spider mites

Red spider mites cause leaves to become yellow-brown and brittle, and a white webbing can be seen on the underside of the leaves of afflicted plants. To get rid of the mites, spray the plant with water, which is their worst enemy.

Scale insects

Scale insects attack both leaves and stems, making them very weak, but are very difficult to detect because of their brownish colour and their stillness. Rub or knock them off the plant with a cottonwool bud dipped in methylated spirit or white spirit.

Plasticine

Plasticine is very useful for fastening slender sprays of foliage to the garden wall; it will last for a long time and is quite waterproof. It can also be used, with or without a stick, to bind up a plant that is bent or partly broken.

Poisonous plants

Anemone: the sap can provoke intense itching.

Buttercup: provokes inflammation of the kidneys and cardiac disorder if eaten.

Conker: the fruit is highly toxic and provokes strong digestive disorders if eaten.

Daffodil: lowers the blood pressure and provokes drowsiness.

Honeysuckle: the berries can be deadly.

Lily of the valley: provokes cardiac disorders and convulsions.

Mistletoe: provokes diarrhoea and cardiac disorders.

Narcissus: the bulb contains poisons.

Snowdrop: the bulb is dangerous, lowers blood pressure and provokes cardiac disorders.

Tulip: the bulb is dangerous, provokes convulsions and cardiac disorders.

Wistaria: the pods are very toxic, and can provoke drowsiness, colic and digestive disorders.

Pots

Plastic pots may be less attractive than clay pots, but they do have advantages: plants in clay pots need more watering, because the clay absorbs the moisture. Plants are as happy in one as in the other.

If you put a plant in a decorative pot, do not forget to place a deep layer of gravel at the bottom to provide drainage, before putting in the compost.

Radishes

Radishes planted near cabbages will discourage maggots.

Roses

To preserve roses for winter, select rosebuds, snip the stem ends and drop the stems into cool melted candlewax or melted sealing wax to cover the end. As soon as the wax is set, wrap each rosebud separately in aluminium foil or greaseproof paper and pack loosely in an airtight box. After sealing the box, store it in a cool place. When the roses are required, unpack them, cut off the waxed end of the stem, stand them in water overnight and they will look as if they have just bloomed.

To revive tired roses, take soot from a chimney or stove where wood has been used as a fuel. Put it into a container, pour boiling water over it and when cold use every day to water the roses. The effect is remarkable: it deepens the colour and produces the rapid growth of shoots. Try with other plants as well.

Rose trees

When planting rose trees, take a patch of grass and place it face downwards at the bottom of the prepared hole. Spread the roots of the rose tree out on it and plant in the usual way. This seems to make the rose trees grow much healthier.

Salsify and scorzonera

For long, straight, healthy-looking salsify, the soil needs to be dug deeply before planting. With only a superficial digging the salsify will grow forked.

Scent

To give a lovely smell to a plant, soak some flower seeds for 2 days in some rose water in which you have infused a small quantity of musk. Leave the seeds to dry a little and then plant them. Water with the same mixture in which they were soaked.

Slugs

A small amount of bran placed around the garden will attract slugs and kill them very quickly.

After squeezing oranges, keep the empty halves and put them in your garden, face down, along a flower bed containing seedlings. Slugs will crawl underneath and can easily be removed each day.

Fill a container with beer and leave it in the garden overnight. In the morning it will be full of slugs.

Thyme

Thyme planted near cabbages and broccoli will discourage cabbage moths.

Houseplants

Buying plants

When buying a houseplant during the cold months of winter, insist on a good wrapping to protect it from the cold when taking it home from the shop.

Do not buy a houseplant from a pavement display outside a shop.

Azalea: when buying an azalea, make sure it is properly moist; at no time should it be allowed to dry out. This can be easily detected by looking at the short woody stem between the soil and the foliage. There should be a dark water mark about half-way up the stem – if the mark is up where the branches begin, it is too wet; if there is no mark at all, it is too dry and you should not buy the plant.

Chrysanthemum: when buying a chrysanthemum, choose it when most of the buds are just opening, never when the buds are tight. A well looked after plant will last for five or six weeks.

Cleaning leaves

Houseplants with hard green leaves (rubber plant, fig tree, philodendron, etc.) should be sponged every 2 or 3 weeks with a piece of cottonwool dipped in milk or flat beer. This will get rid of dust, allow the leaves to breathe more freely and make them look glossy and green.

The use of oil is not recommended, as it clogs the pores of the leaves and makes it harder for them to breathe.

Colour

Houseplant flowers will have a deeper colour if the plant is watered with sooty water from time to time. This also applies to garden flowers.

Feeding

Plants have a dormant period (September to April or May) so do not feed them during that time as they are practically inactive. Also, do not water them as often as during the summer months.

Do not feed plants when they are in full bloom.

Most plants develop their new growth in the spring, so feeding should start in spring and continue until early autumn.

Home-grown plants

For children

Children enjoy growing their own houseplants, so let them experiment with the following. Cut the tops off fresh carrots, beetroots, turnips, parsnips, etc. and stand them on a dinner plate with enough water to cover the bottom section. Put the plate in a light place and keep the base moist. Shoots will appear after a few days, and leaves after about a week. The carrots will have feathery leaves, and the beetroots and turnips will have red veined leaves.

Plants from seeds

Avocado: an avocado makes a lovely leathery-leafed plant. Put an

avocado stone, pointed end uppermost, in a glass filled with water or a pot filled with compost, leaving half the stone above the surface. If using water, push three or four toothpicks into the side of the stone and rest them on the rim of the glass as a support. Keep in a warm place which is not too light until shoots appear, and then move to a lighter place. Transplant into sandy soil when the roots become strong.

Citrus fruit: orange, lemon, grapefruit, tangerine and lime all form plants with small, shiny dark-green leaves. Plant a few pips to germinate together in moist compost about half an inch or 1 cm deep. Keep in a warm dark place until shoots appear, then re-pot singly when they are about 3 or 4 inches long (about 7 to 10 centimetres).

Date: a date can make a strong and most attractive palm. Take some fresh date stones and put them to germinate in moist compost about half an inch or 1 cm deep, with the pointed end uppermost. Keep in a warm dark place with constantly damp soil until shoots appear, then bring the pot into the light, keeping the soil moist.

Pineapple: for a hardy and very attractive green plant, cut off the top of a pineapple at the base of the tuft. Scoop out the flesh and put the base in a vase containing water, or in a pot of moist, sandy compost. Leave in a light, warm place. Roots will develop at the base, the leaves will grow longer and stronger every day, and new leaves will appear. For the best results, choose a pineapple with healthy leaves.

Plants from leaves

African violet: this can be propagated by cutting a leaf with its stem and planting it in a pot of compost. Mother-in-law's tongue, dragon plant and pepper elder can also be propagated in this way.

Begonia: this can be propagated by leaf planting or vein cutting. Take a fully grown leaf with very prominent veins and make a few small incisions in the biggest veins on the underside. Place the leaf, shiny side up, on damp compost. Weight it with small stones, cover the pot with a piece of transparent plastic and place in indirect sunlight. Roots will form where the incisions were made; shoots will grow from them, and when they are big enough they can be potted separately.

Sanseviera: this can be propagated simply by cutting the leaves into sections (use a sharp knife) and planting each section in a pot. Do not water too much or the plant will rot.

Poisonous plants

Some common houseplants are poisonous if eaten. Be particularly careful when there are children and animals around.

Azalea: the whole plant is toxic and provokes colic.

Cyclamen: the whole plant is toxic and causes violent headaches and convulsions.

Dieffenbachia: the whole plant is venomous and the sap is toxic.

Philodendron: the plant can provoke intoxication.

Poinsettia: the corrosive sap can provoke diarrhoea, cramp and delirium.

Primrose: the plant can provoke curious allergies.

Solanium (pommes d'amour): the whole plant is toxic.

Watering

Growth takes place in spring and summer, and plants need a lot of watering during this time.

Growth is slow in winter and plants need less water, but a certain amount of watering is still necessary, particularly if you have central heating.

If a plant is absorbing water very quickly, it probably needs a larger pot. Check the roots: if they are compressed, the pot is too small.

A plant with yellow, falling leaves has been over-watered; allow it to dry out for a few days.

A plant with a limp stem and dropping leaves needs watering badly. Plunge the whole pot into a container of water and leave it submerged until the last bubble comes to the surface, then drain.

To test if a plant needs watering, leave a pebble on top of the soil: if the underside is still damp when you turn the pebble over, the plant does not need water; if it is dry, it does. Alternatively, insert a skewer or pencil in the soil: if it comes out with damp soil attached to it, it still does not need watering; if it comes out clean, it does. (Soil can appear dry on the surface but be moist underneath).

To keep soil moist longer and to avoid evaporation, cover the surface of the pot with pebbles, gravel or moss.

A little watering from time to time is not enough, and will make the roots turn upwards to reach the water. A successful method with most plants is to plunge them into a bucket of water (the whole pot must be submerged) until bubbles of air stop coming to the surface. Drain carefully.

Do not leave pots standing in a saucer of water as this causes the roots to rot.

Most plants can be watered from the top, except for cyclamen, African violets and peperomia – if these corms were submerged under water, the buds or young leaves could be damaged. Stand the pot in 2 inches (4 cm) of water for half an hour or until the surface of the soil shows moisture. This method of watering should also be used for plants with delicate leaves and flowers.

All plants like to have their foliage sprayed, except for furry-leafed plants like African violets. Spray plants often as this keeps humidity in the air, which is perfect for the plants to thrive in.

When you are planning to go away and there is nobody to water your plants, soak the soil thoroughly and, while still dripping, put the plant and pot in a polythene bag. Close the bag and put the wrapped plant in a good position where it will get indirect daylight. When you come home after three or four weeks, the plant will be as happy as when you left it and still quite damp.

Another method of long-term watering is to take a piece of bandage, put one end in a bowl of water and tuck the other end into the soil. The bandage will draw water from the bowl into the soil.

Philodendron: if a philodendron develops aerial roots instead of winding them around on top of the soil in the pot, direct the roots into a container of water. The plant will take moisture from this source and the soil in the pot will need very little watering.

Window boxes

Scented herbs such as parsley, chervil, thyme, chives, marjoram and rosemary are very good as window-box plants. Keep them well moistened.

An easy way to keep your boxes looking lovely is to fill them with plants in their pots, packing some soil around the pots. This makes it easier either to remove a plant if it is not doing well, or to take all the plants inside during cold weather. (They can be put back later when the weather improves.)

To keep your boxes in bloom all season, remove the dead flower heads as soon as they die. This, of course, also applies to garden flowers.

General hints

Baby oil

A few drops of baby oil in your bath water will stop your skin becoming dry.

Bathing cap

To prevent water penetrating your bathing cap, wear a narrow band of chamois leather under it.

Bath oil

To make perfumed bath oil at home, mix ½ pint (300 ml) of almond oil with ½ pint (300 ml) of olive oil. Add 10 drops of essence of jasmine – or the perfume of your choice – and shake well.

Breath

Bad breath can quickly be remedied by crunching a clove. Your breath will have the scent of a carnation.

If your breath smells of garlic, chew a coffee bean or a stalk of parsley or celery.

Cheeks

To shade your cheeks, apply shading powder over your face powder. Suck in your cheeks to find your natural hollow and then brush on the shading powder, starting from inside the hollow and moving outwards to the hairline.

Cigarette stains

To get rid of nicotene stains, rub your fingers with quarter of a lemon or with cottonwool dipped in peroxide. Rinse your fingers immediately.

Complexion

For a good complexion drink five glasses of water a day. Let it become a habit: it will ensure good elimination and therefore encourage a good complexion.

If you have lost your youthful complexion, drink five glasses of water a day, and every morning before breakfast drink the juice of half a lemon in hot water (you will get to like it). Before going to bed, drink a cup of hot skimmed milk, mixed with ½ tablespoon of wheatgerm.

Start your meal with a green salad. Eat lean meat, grilled or roasted. Use artificial sweetener instead of sugar. If you follow this diet for at least a week every month, your complexion and figure will improve greatly.

To give a bloom to your complexion when tired, mix a few drops of liquid blusher with your liquid foundation and make up your face with it.

Eau de cologne

Cologne contains more alcohol than eau de toilette (toilet water) but is cooler and more refreshing. It is weaker than eau de toilette, and perfect for providing a light touch of scent. It is good for teenagers.

Eau de toilette

Toilet water contains a higher percentage of alcohol than concentrated perfume. It evaporates more quickly and the fragrance does not last as long as perfume, but it is more refreshing. It should be sprayed over your body and around the neck.

Eyebrows

To keep the hairs in place, stroke them with a small brush dampened with hair lacquer.

When plucking eyebrows, you should pluck below and between if necessary but never above as this would alter their natural shape.

Eyebrows are the frames of your eyes: do not shave or pluck out all your eyebrows as they will grow back very untidily. Very rarely does a picture look its best without a frame.

Eyes

Eye make-up for women who wear glasses: if you wear glasses for short-sightedness, the eye make-up needs to be a little stronger. On the other hand, glasses for long-sightedness make the eyes look bigger so eye make-up should be light.

Puffy eyes: reduce the swelling by applying a pad of cottonwool dampened in iced water to each eye, leaving it on until the pad becomes warm. Another method is to use a teabag dipped in cold water, or apply thin slices of raw potato.

Face cream

Liquid paraffin is as good as any face cream and much, much cheaper. Dab here and there, massage upwards into the skin and wipe off the surplus. It will leave your skin very smooth.

Face steam

To clear the skin, put a handful of fresh peppermint leaves in a bowl and cover with boiling water. Immediately put your face over the bowl, cover your head and the bowl with a large towel, and steam your face for as long as the steam lasts. Then dry with a clean pad. Peppermint is antiseptic and stimulates the circulation.

False eyelashes

When new, soak false eyelashes for a few minutes in warm water. This will remove the stiffness and make them more supple and natural-looking.

Feet

To soothe tired feet, first walk on tiptoes for a few minutes, then shower them with water as hot as you can take it for 2 minutes. Follow with cold water for 1 minute and then dry energetically, going up the ankles.

Hair

To intensify light tones in naturally blonde hair, use a strong infusion of camomile flowers for the final rinse. Infuse 2 handfuls of camomile flowers in 1 pint or 500ml water for 30 minutes. Let it cool a little before use.

To make hair silky and easy to comb, add a little wine vinegar to the last rinse. It will remove any traces of soap left in the hair.

Hand care

If you have been doing heavy work without gloves on, make a paste with a potato peeled and boiled in water, 1 teaspoon of glycerine and the juice of a lemon. Rub your hands with the paste for a few minutes and then rinse. Repeat this treatment a few times during the day. Your hands will become smooth again.

For an everyday hand treatment, mix equal parts of eau de cologne, rose water, glycerine and lemon juice.

Lipstick

Powder your lips before putting on your lipstick: it will look neater and stay that way.

Dark-red lipstick makes you look older, light colours make you look younger. Orange-red can be flattering, but it hardens the features and really suits only the exotic type. Orange and rusty colours emphasise yellow teeth.

Make-up

If you have wrinkles, blow out your cheeks when you powder your face; look up when powdering underneath your eyes.

When applying a product to your face with your hands or when cleansing with tissues, always proceed from the bottom to the top. Movements from top to bottom provoke sagging skin and wrinkles.

When applying coloured foundation to your face, dot it on first, then take some cottonwool dipped in rose water and carefully spread the product all over your face. Using this method, you will obtain a uniform make-up which will last longer.

To find out if you are using the right foundation for your skin type, pour some water into a glass, put a drop of foundation on your fingertip and touch the surface of the water. If the foundation dissolves, it is oil in water and suitable for an oily skin; if it stays on your finger, it is water in oil and suitable for a dry skin.

To keep make-up fresh all day or all evening, dip a pad of cottonwool in water and squeeze out the excess moisture. When you have made up your face, dab the pad over your powdered skin and it will set the powder for many hours with no need for retouching.

For evening, a light touch of pearly white face powder on the cheekbones, the middle of the forehead and underneath the eyebrows will give a glow to your face.

Masks

For an older skin

Warm some olive oil in a bowl which is standing in hot water; soak in it a piece of cottonwool large enough to cover your face. Protect your eyes with pads of cottonwool dampened with water, then place the oily piece of cottonwool on your face and keep it on until cold. Cleanse your face with soft tissues, then pat with cottonwool dampened in cold water.

Monthly masks

The following beauty masks can be used once a month to clean your face: they will cleanse the skin of all the impurities which block the pores. These masks should be put on a clean skin after cleansing and toning; do not put on your eyelids or under your eyes. Remove the mask with cottonwool dipped in warm water.

For greasy skin: dilute 2 teaspoons of cornflour with one lightly beaten egg white and mix until creamy but not too thick. Apply gently to your face and leave to dry. When your skin starts to pull strongly, rinse with warm water.

*For dry and delicate skin:*make a thin paste with the yolk of an egg, some orange juice, and a few drops of lemon juice and almond oil. Apply the mask to your face, leave it on for 15 minutes and then remove with warm water.

For all types of skin: yogurt makes a good, relaxing mask which leaves your face soft and fresh-looking.

Nails

Do not cut your nails with scissors as this can cause them to split. File them with an emery board, which is softer than a metal file.

To make your nails look longer, do not cover the entire surface of the nail with varnish but leave a space on each side.

When you are doing a dirty job without gloves on, scratch a piece of soap with your nails. The soap will stay under your nails and prevent them from becoming caked with dirt.

Nose

If your nose goes red and has a burning sensation, rub your ears firmly with your hands. The blood will rush to your ears and leave your nose.

Parsley

Parsley has a high Vitamin A content which is good for the skin, so eat as much of it as possible.

Perfume

Perfume is very expensive and very strong, so do not shower yourself with it. A dab behind each ear, in the crook of each elbow, and on the inside of your wrists – and sometimes a few dabs around the inside of the hem of your skirt – is quite sufficient.

When opened, keep the bottle in a cool place in the dark. When exposed to light and heat, perfume becomes rusty and loses its scent.

Powder

Apply loose powder over foundation with a powder puff, or open a pad of cottonwool, place some powder in the middle, close the pad and apply generously to the face. Brush off the excess with a tissue or very soft brush.

Powder should be one shade lighter than the foundation, or translucent, so as not to affect the colour of the foundation.

Pressed powder in compacts is good for retouching your face during the day or evening.

Shampoo

When brushing dry shampoo out of your hair, put a piece of gauze over the bristles of the hairbrush to absorb dirt and oil.

Sunbathing

The most dangerous time of the day for sunbathing is between 11 a.m. and 2 p.m. At this time, the sun is at its strongest and therefore more likely to burn the skin.

Beware of a deep suntan. It makes the features look harder and deepens lines, thus ageing the face.

Sunbathing preparations containing oil of bergamot can leave patches on the skin: they will fade with the tan, but will reappear as strongly as soon as one is in the sun again. This is because oil of bergamot accelerates the pigmentation of the skin under ultra-violet rays, making the skin tan more quickly but very often patchily because the skin's pigmentation is irregular. As oil of bergamot is an ingredient in perfume, it is not recommended that you use perfume before sunbathing.

Sunburn

For immediate relief, apply a compress dipped in a mixture of water and vinegar. Use 5 tablespoons of vinegar to 1 pint (½ litre) of water.

Suntan oil

To sunbathe without burning, fill a small bottle with refined, odourless olive oil and add a few drops of tincture of iodine (available from chemists). Shaken well and used on your skin when sunbathing, it will give a lovely golden tan.

Walking

You will walk twice as far and be less tired if you shift your weight from the heel to the ball of your front foot – your body will be lighter and the weight will be distributed naturally and more evenly over the joints. It will make a big difference to your health and efficiency.

It is also important to wear comfortable shoes.

Water

Water on your face should never be left to dry by itself. Dry it immediately, because dampness, if left too long, irritates the skin of your face (as it does the hands).

General hints

This section is not intended to suggest that all complaints can or should be treated in the home. Any acute or recurrent ailments should, of course, be treated by a doctor. The following hints are for minor aches and pains, or for times when you cannot see the doctor immediately and want some temporary relief.

Ankles

To relieve swollen ankles, chop some ivy leaves and secure round the ankles with a bandage, leaving for a few hours. If the swelling persists or recurs, consult a doctor.

Apples

Apples increase the fibre content in your diet, which improves the efficiency of bowel action and can prevent constipation and other bowel disorders. Eat an apple a day, washed but not peeled. For small children who cannot chew, grate the apple or puree it in an electric blender.

Artificial respiration

If the patient is not breathing, put him on his back, support the nape of his neck, tilt his head back and press his chin up to stop his tongue blocking the air in the throat.

Mouth-to-mouth resuscitation

The above procedure should start the patient breathing again – if not, start mouth-to-mouth resuscitation: pinch his nostrils with your fingers, open your mouth, take a deep breath and seal your lips around the patient's mouth. Blow into the lungs until his chest rises, then remove your mouth and watch his chest falling. Continue doing

this 12 times each minute until professional help arrives. When the patient is a child, mouth-to-mouth resuscitation should be done by sealing your lips around his nose and mouth and blowing gently into his mouth 16 to 18 times a minute.

Heart massage

If, despite mouth-to-mouth resuscitation, the patient starts turning a blue-grey colour, start heart massage. The patient should be on his back: place yourself on one side, and put the heel of your hand on the lower half of the breastbone with the palm and fingers off the chest. Cover this hand with the heel of your other hand and, with straight arms, press down on the lower half of the breastbone in a rocking motion. For an adult do 15 heart compressions, followed by two lung inflations; for children do 10 compressions, applying much lighter pressure with only one hand, about 70 times a minute. Every 20 compressions do two inflations, being careful not to be too violent in case you break a rib.

Asthma

Games which involve blowing and taking deep breaths, such as blowing soap bubbles, are good for children with asthma.

Bleeding

To stop bleeding, lay a handful of flour on the cut or dredge it with some freshly ground pepper. This will also act as a disinfectant.

Boils

To make an ointment for boils, mix together 1 dessertspoon each of honey, olive oil and flour. Beat the yolk of an egg and mix it with the other ingredients. Spread this on gauze and put it on the boil. Renew the application every 6 hours: it will draw out the core after the boil has broken. If the boil recurs, consult a doctor.

Boots

Wellington boots can be cold in winter: a few layers of newspaper cut to the shape of the sole and placed inside the boots will insulate your feet and keep them warm.

Bran

Buy unprocessed bran from a health-food shop or chemist. One teaspoonful before each meal is the best and the cheapest way of correcting constipation and diarrhoea. Alternatively, mix 2 heaped teaspoons of the bran into your breakfast cereal, which makes it easier to swallow.

Bruises

To prevent bruises, take a little dry arrowroot or dry starch, moisten it with cold water and apply to the injured part as soon as possible. The sooner this is done after the injury takes place the more effective it will be.

Burns

For a small burn, hold the affected part under running cold water for a while.

For burns caused by household alkalis (e.g. ammonia, washing soda, borax, etc.), wash the burn with water and apply lemon juice or vinegar to stop the effect of the alkali on the skin.

For burns caused by chemicals, the chemical should be removed before the burn is immersed in water as some chemicals react violently with water.

Cabbage

Cabbage is the medicine of the poor, with many healing virtues.

For gout, rheumatism, arthritis, sciatica or muscular pains, take some large cabbage leaves, cut out the hard middle vein and gently press the leaves with a medium-warm iron until they soften. Apply a few layers of the warm leaves to the sore part, securing them with a bandage or plaster. Renew twice a day.

For burns, insect bites, swellings and cuts, cabbage acts as a mild disinfectant. Clean the leaves very carefully, press them with a medium-warm iron and apply to the affected area. Crushed cabbage leaves can also be used.

Cabbage water

For sore throats, chop some cabbage leaves (any variety), put them in a pan, pour on boiling water, cover and leave to infuse for 10 minutes. Strain the infusion and gargle with it. Repeat this operation every 2 hours.

Cherries

Do not give drinks to children when they are eating cherries or any other soft fruit. The liquid causes the pulp to swell and makes it heavy on the stomach.

Children

If your child eats too quickly, give him only small quantities of food on his plate, and a small fork and a small spoon instead of adult cutlery.

A child will take his medicine more readily if you pour it into a glass and stir it so that it becomes frothy.

Choking

If a person chokes on a piece of food, act quickly. Bang him hard between the shoulder blades or, if this doesn't help, grasp him round the waist from behind, one fist clenched with the thumb towards the stomach. Clasp this fist with the other hand – the hands should be above the navel, below the rib cage – and then give a sudden squeeze, pushing the clenched fist into the upper stomach with a lifting motion. The piece of food should pop out after one or two hugs.

If a child under the age of four chokes, hold him up by his legs and bang him between the shoulders. If the child is older, put him over your knees, head downwards and slap him between the shoulders.

Cold

Smelling salts are a great help in unblocking the nose.

Compress

For a cold compress, put some ice-cubes and methylated spirit (5 tablespoons to 1 pint or 500ml) into water and dip in a piece of linen or a face-towel. The evaporation of the spirit will keep the compress cold for longer. It should not be used near the eyes.

Cramp

A towel dipped in hot water and applied to the cramp will bring immediate relief.

For cramp in the leg, simultaneously stretch out the heel and draw up the toes as far as possible.

Diabetics

If a diabetic begins to tremble, sweat or act aggressively, it may be caused by too much, or not enough, sugar in the bloodstream. If he is able to swallow (an unconscious person should not be given anything by mouth) give plenty of sugar dissolved in a warm drink, or in lumps, or 2 tablespoons of powered sugar. If the condition was caused by too little sugar the patient will improve immediately; if there is no improvement, the sugar will not have done any harm but the person should be taken to hospital or a doctor should be called.

Earache

A doctor should be consulted for earache, but temporary relief may be obtained by resting the ear on a covered hot-water bottle.

Temporary relief may also be obtained by putting a few drops of lukewarm oil, either olive oil or ordinary cooking oil, in the ear.

Electric shock

The longer a person is attached to the current, the worse his condition will become. Switch off the current and remove the plug. If this is not possible the person must be pulled away, but first insulate yourself or the shock will pass on to you if you touch him with bare hands, anything metal or anything damp. Wrap newspaper round your hand or use an object made of wood (a broom will do) or rubber to pull the victim clear. If he is suffering from burns, immerse the burned part in cool water, never oil or cream. If he isn't breathing, give artificial respiration and call a doctor.

Eyes

Inflamed eyes should be treated by a doctor, but temporary relief may be obtained in the following way. Chop some clean parsley very finely, use it to fill two thin muslin bags large enough to cover the eyes, and tack the open end. Lie down with a bowl of cold water next to you, dip the bags in it and lay them on the eyes. Turn them from time to time and dip them in water again when they become warm. Do this for 15 minutes.

Fainting

To help the blood return to the brain, bend the head down to the knees. Then lay the patient down flat.

An emergency method to help you stop fainting in a hot or stuffy atmosphere is to dig your fingernail firmly into the space between your nose and upper lip.

Giddiness

To counteract giddiness, drink about 2 tablespoons of pure lemon juice.

Hangover

To avoid a hangover, drink several glasses of water before going to bed.

Headache

A soupspoon of lemon juice will often relieve a bilious headache. A glass of soda water is often effective, too.

A headache caused by foods which have fermented (e.g. chocolate, yoghurt, cheese, etc.) or drinks such as beer, whisky, red wine or gin can be helped by taking as much honey as you like, a small quantity at a time.

Hiccups

To stop hiccups, eat a small piece of ice.

Drink a glass of water, holding a knife blade down in the glass.

Marigold

For wounds or skin eruptions, soak a marigold in salad oil and apply the petals. The oil will help the wound to heal more quickly.

Medicine

To avoid the taste of unpleasant medicine, eat a strong peppermint just before taking it, or suck an ice-cube.

The medicine cabinet is usually in the bathroom, but burns and cuts

most often occur in the kitchen so keep some ointment there as well.
Remember to keep medicine locked away and out of the reach of
children.

Nose bleeds

Seat the patient with his head leaning forward and with the thumb
pressed firmly on the bleeding nostril. Continue this treatment for at
least 10 minutes. If this does not stop the bleeding, put a piece of
cottonwool dipped in peroxide in the bleeding nostril.

Nostrils

Breathe through your nostrils and not through your mouth: the
nostrils and sinuses are lined with tiny cells and hairs which catch the
dust and prevent it reaching the lungs.

Patients

Keep patients entertained by giving them a view of the outside world:
hang a mirror in such a way that it reflects through the window.

Pills

An easy way to swallow a pill is to place it under the tongue and then
take a big mouthful of water. Water and pill will go down together
easily.

Poisoning

If children (or adults) are poisoned by household products, do not
panic; note the time immediately.

Do not make the patient vomit if he is not completely conscious.

Do not make the patient vomit if he has swallowed foaming or
caustic products, or petrol-based products. Foaming or caustic
products include caustic soda, bleach, potassium chlorate and
strong acids; petrol-based products include methylated spirit, white
spirit and dry-cleaning fluid.

If the patient does vomit, lie him on his side.

If the patient has swallowed a foaming product, do not give him anything to drink for many hours. If it was bleach, make him drink water to dilute the product and make it less caustic.

If the poison taken is a foaming or caustic product, empty the stomach by giving the patient a cupful of warm water mixed with 1 teaspoon of mustard (dry or fresh), or put your fingers down his throat.

Take the patient to the hospital without delay, also taking the container of poisonous product.

Rheumatism

Warmth is very comforting during an attack of rheumatism. Apply a hot-water bottle, wrapped in a towel to avoid burning. Fill the bottle only half full so that it can be wrapped around the affected parts.

Salt

Do not put too much salt on your fresh vegetables, as this causes water retention which will swell your tissues. Salt can be replaced with chives.

To relieve a cold or hayfever, take dry salt in the same manner as snuff.

Wash your teeth and rinse your mouth with salt water. It makes your teeth white, sweetens the breath and hardens the gums.

After tooth extraction, rinse with salt water to stop the bleeding.

Shellfish

Shellfish poached in vinegar and water does not give nettle rash.

Sneezing

To stop a sneeze, touch your palate firmly with the tip of your tongue.

Splinters

To extract a splinter quickly from a hand, especially a child's, place the affected part over a jar or wide-mouthed bottle half filled with very hot water. If a little pressure is used, the steam will induce the extraction of the splinter.

Stings

For a bee or wasp sting, wash the area with a mixture of 1 tablespoon of vinegar and half a glass of water. Then apply a slice of raw onion, which will ease the pain and reduce the swelling.

To stop the poison spreading, apply a piece of ice to the sting. If the swelling continues, consult a doctor.

To relieve a nettle sting, rub the area with rosemary, mint or sage leaves.

Thermometers

Don't put a thermometer in a young child's mouth, as he might bite and break it. The thermometer should be tucked first under the arm and then into the groin with the knees bent up into the tummy, which should give an accurate reading of the child's temperature.

Toenails

Clip your toenails straight across, using nail clippers. This is very important to avoid ingrowing nails, which are very painful.

For ingrowing toenails, cut a notch in the middle of the nail. The natural tendency to close the notch will draw the nail away from the sides.

Toothache

Temporary relief may be obtained by placing a clove inside the mouth on the affected area.

Toothbrushes

Nylon toothbrushes are good for your teeth. The texture can easily be changed by putting the brush into cold water to harden it, or into hot water to soften it. Natural bristles are hollow, so they accumulate water and can be a breeding ground for germs.

Vitamin C

Do not prepare your orange juice in advance, as contact with the air will destroy the Vitamin C.

Warts

To get rid of a wart, apply nail varnish once a day. Regular treatment should cause the wart to dry up and disappear after a period of time.

Weight

When weight-watching, remember to weigh yourself every morning. Adjust your day's food intake accordingly.

Index

African violet, growing from leaves, 126;
  watering, 128
alabaster, cleaning and maintenance, 64
almonds, skinning, 13; storage time, 53
aluminium, 64
amber, cleaning and maintenance, 65
ammonia, as cleaning agent, 61
anchovies, preparation, 13
ankles, swollen, 143
ants, garden, 115
apples, 13, 143; see also fruit
apple stains, 13
arrowroot, in cookery, 13
arthritis, cabbage compress for, 146
artichokes, globe, 13-14
artificial respiration, 143-4
ash, cigarette, 65; for cleaning polished tables,
  111; wood, for cleaning aluminium, 64
asparagus, 14; serving quantities, 58
asthma, 144
aubergines, preparation, 14-15
avocados, 15; growing as houseplant, 125-6
azalea, 124

baby oil, for dry skin, 133
bacon, 15; storage time, 55
bad breath, 133
bags, stained, 65
bamboo, cleaning, 65
bananas, 15; see also fruit
barbecues, 15
barrels, cleaning, 65
basil, 15-16; see also herbs
bathing caps, 133
bath oil, making, 133
baths, stained, 65
bay leaves, drying and storing, 16
beads, threading, 65-6
beans, dried, 16; see also vegetables
beef, 16-17; see also meat
beef broth, making, 17
beer, in cookery, 17; marinade for beef and
  poultry, 35; with fish, 28
beetroot, 17
begonia, growing from leaves, 126
bergamot, oil of, in sunbathing preparations, 139

bicarbonate of soda, as cleaning agent, 61
biscuits, crumbly, buttering, 45
blackcurrants, 17
bleach smells, 66
bleeding, 145; gums, use of salt, 151; nose, 150
boils, ointment for, 145
bone, repairing cracks in, 81
bones, left-over, 18
books, cleaning and repairing, 66
boots, to insulate, 145
bottles, 67; cleaning, 172; drying, 72-3; plastic,
  disposal of, 90
bouillon, making and storing, 18
bouquet garni, making, 18
bran, 145; as cleaning agent, 67; for cleaning
  jewellery, 82; for preserving grapes, 31
brass, cleaning, 67
bread, 18
breathing, 150
bronze, cleaning, 67
browning, for bouillon, 19
brushes, cleaning, 68
Brussels sprouts, 19
burns, 145
burnt food, on pans, 88
butter, 19
buttons, sewing on thick material, 92

cabbage, 19; growing, 115-16; medicinal uses,
  146; serving quantities, 58
cakes, preparation and baking, 19-20
candles, 68
cane, cleaning and maintenance, 68
canvas, sewing, 75
capsicum, peeling, 32
caramel, to prevent hardening, 20
carpets, to prevent edges curling, 85
carrot fly, 116
carrot juice, 20
carrots, cleaning, 20; growing, 116; serving
  quantities, 58
cauliflower, 19; growing, 115-16
celery flowers, making, 44
celery leaves, uses, 20
cereals, storage times, 52